THE
ROBERT LOUIS STEVENSON
TRAIL

A WALKING TOUR IN THE VELAY AND CÉVENNES, SOUTHERN FRANCE

About the Author

Alan Castle has trekked in over 30 countries within Europe, Asia, North and South America, Africa and Australasia, and for 17 years led organised walking holidays in several European countries. A member of the British Outdoor Writers and Photographers Guild, he has written more than a dozen walking guidebooks, several on long-distance mountain routes in France. His longer solo walks include a 'grand traverse' of the European Alps between Nice and Vienna (2430km/ 1510 miles), the Pilgrim's Trail from Le Puy to Santiago de Compostela (1545km/960 miles) and a coast-to-coast route across the French Pyrenees (870km/ 540 miles). A Munroist, and erstwhile national secretary and long-distance-path information officer of the Long Distance Walkers Association, Alan now lives at the foot of the Moffat Hills in Scotland, in the heart of the Southern Uplands.

In 1988 Alan first walked the trail taken by the Scottish writer, Robert Louis Stevenson, through the Velay and Cévennes of southern France. This was 110 years after Stevenson's visit. As a result, he became addicted to the area, visiting many times over the ensuing years to walk many hundreds of kilometres of the region's trails, including the ultra-long GR4, as well as the circular *tours* of the Velay, Cévennes, Mont Lozère and Mont Aigoual, and long trails in the Causses. By bicycle, he has completed the 666km (410 mile) Grande Traversée du Massif Central right across the region.

Alan's continuing fascination with the life and works of RL Stevenson has taken him around the world following in the author's footsteps, including a visit to Western Samoa to pay homage at the grave of the great man, on a hill above Vailima.

Other guidebooks by Alan Castle for Cicerone

Tour of the Queyras (French and Italian Alps), 1990, new edition 2008
Walks In Volcano Country (Auvergne and the Velay), 1992
Walking the French Gorges (Provence and the Ardèche), 1993
The Brittany Coastal Path, 1995
Walking in the Ardennes, 1996
The River Rhine Trail, 1999
Walking in Bedfordshire, 2001
The John Muir Trail, 2004
The Southern Upland Way, 2007
Alan was also the author for Cicerone of the first and second editions of *The Corsican High Level Route* (1987, 1992) and *A Pyrenean Trail (GR10)* (1990, 1997)

THE
ROBERT LOUIS STEVENSON
TRAIL

A WALKING TOUR IN THE VELAY AND CÉVENNES, SOUTHERN FRANCE

by
Alan Castle

2 POLICE SQUARE, MILNTHORPE, CUMBRIA LA7 7PY
www.cicerone.co.uk

Second edition 2007
ISBN-13: 978-1-85284-511-7

First edition 1992
ISBN-10: 1-85284-060-9

> For my part, I travel not to go anywhere, but to go.
> I travel for travel's sake. The great affair is to move.
> *Travels with a Donkey* RL Stevenson,1879

Dedication
Dedicated to all who would follow in the footsteps of
Stevenson and Modestine

For Dad Cain (1932–2000)

Acknowledgements

I am indebted to Pat Valette of Club Cévenol for encouragement, advice and local information, both in the preparation of the first edition of this guidebook, published in 1992, and during the research and writing of this completely revised second edition.

My wife, Beryl Castle, has always over the years given freely of her advice, support and encouragement during the planning, research and writing of my guidebooks, and this book was no exception. For this I am ever grateful, and also for her help in the preparation of the sketch maps for this book.

I also wish to thank Club Cévenol, Mainstream Publishing (Edinburgh) and Gordon Golding for permission to quote from RL Stevenson's *The Cévennes Journal*.

Finally, I thank Jonathan Williams and his staff at Cicerone Press for their professionalism in publishing this and my other guidebooks.

Front cover: Old bridge crossing the River Tarn at Le Pont de Montvert (Stage 8)

CONTENTS

Advice to Readers

Readers are advised that while every effort is taken by the author to ensure the accuracy of this guidebook, changes can occur which may affect the contents. It is advisable to check locally on transport, accommodation, shops, etc., but even rights of way can be altered.

The publisher would welcome notes of any such changes.

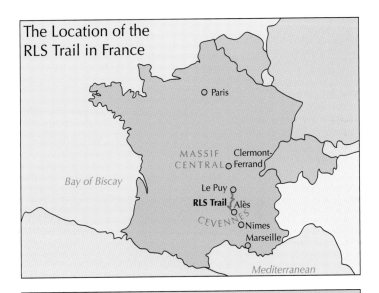

The Location of the RLS Trail in France

O Paris

MASSIF
CENTRAL O Clermont-Ferrand

Bay of Biscay

Le Puy O
RLS Trail O Alès
CEVENNES
O Nîmes
Marseille

Mediterranean

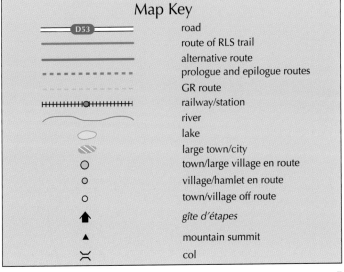

Map Key

D53	road
	route of RLS trail
	alternative route
	prologue and epilogue routes
	GR route
╫╫╫╫●╫╫╫╫	railway/station
	river
	lake
	large town/city
O	town/large village en route
o	village/hamlet en route
o	town/village off route
♠	*gîte d'étapes*
▲	mountain summit
⨉	col

TRAIL GUIDE – SUMMARY TABLE OF STAGES

		Distance km	Distance miles	Est Time hr min
PROLOGUE	Le Puy-en-Velay to Le Monastier-sur-Gazeille	19.1	11.9	5 15
STAGE 1	Le Monastier-sur-Gazeille to Goudet	10.2	6.3	3 00
STAGE 2	Goudet to Le Bouchet-Saint-Nicolas	12.8	8.0	3 40
	Excursion to Lac du Bouchet	10.0	6.2	2 45
STAGE 3	Le Bouchet-Saint-Nicolas to Pradelles	21.0	13.0	5 10
STAGE 4	Pradelles to Langogne	6.4	4.0	1 35
STAGE 5	Langogne to Cheylard-l'Évêque	15.8	9.8	4 10
STAGE 6	Cheylard-l'Évêque via Notre-Dame-des-Neiges to La Bastide-Puylaurent	23.4	14.5	7 00
STAGE 7	La Bastide-Puylaurent to Les Alpiers/Le Bleymard	26.1/28.0	16.2/17.4	7 20 / 7 55
STAGE 8	Les Alpiers/Le Bleymard to Le Pont-de-Montvert	21.1/19.2	13.1/11.9	6 35 / 6 00
STAGE 9	Le Pont-de-Montvert to Florac	27.3	17.0	8 45
STAGE 10	Florac to Gare de Cassagnas	17.4	10.8	5 00
STAGE 11	Gare de Cassagnas to Saint-Germain-de-Calberte	13.6	8.5	4 45
STAGE 12	Saint-Germain-de-Calberte To Saint-Jean-du-Gard	21.4	13.3	7 15
EPILOGUE	Saint-Jean-du-Gard to Mialet	6.0	3.7	1 50
	Mialet to Alès	20.0	12.4	8 15
TOTALS	**Le Monastier-sur-Gazeille to Saint-Jean-du-Gard**	**226.5**	**140.7**	**67 00**
	Le Puy to Alès	**271.6**	**168.7**	**82 20**

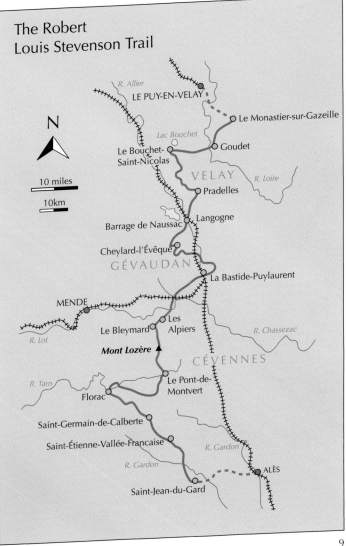

The Robert
Louis Stevenson Trail

N

10 miles
10km

R. Allier

LE PUY-EN-VELAY

Le Monastier-sur-Gazeille

Lac Bouchet

Le Bouchet-
Saint-Nicolas

Goudet

VELAY

R. Loire

Pradelles

Langogne

Barrage de Naussac

Cheylard-l'Évêque

GÉVAUDAN

La Bastide-Puylaurent

MENDE

Les
Alpiers

Le Bleymard

R. Lot

R. Chassezac

Mont Lozère

CÉVENNES

R. Tarn

Le Pont-de-
Montvert

Florac

Saint-Germain-de-Calberte

Saint-Étienne-Vallée-Francaise

R. Gardon

R. Gardon

ALÈS

Saint-Jean-du-Gard

9

The Château de Beaufort and the River Loire at Goudet (Stage 1)

PREFACE TO THE SECOND EDITION

Back in 1988, when I first walked the Robert Louis Stevenson Trail from Le Monastier-sur-Gazeille in the Velay to Saint-Jean-du-Gard in the Cévennes, following in the footsteps of the 19th-century Scottish writer, the situation was very different from that found today. The trail was an unofficial one, and very few people walked the route. I met no other walkers on my journey and I was almost certainly the only person from the UK to walk the trail that year. The locals could not understand why I was walking there, and nobody I talked to had even heard of RL Stevenson!

All that has now changed entirely. In 1994 the trail was adopted by the Fédération Française de la Randonnée Pédestre, who christened it the GR70, but not before making very considerable changes. The new, much-improved trail has far less road walking than the earlier route, but it still links up all the villages and towns I passed through on my first visit in 1988, and most that Stevenson visited in 1878. During that first year of the official 'Chemin de Stevenson', it was said that about 200 walkers used it. Nowadays it has become one of France's most popular long-distance trails, with an estimated 6000 hikers per annum walking its full length.

In 1988 the regions through which I passed were much in need of revitalisation. The villages tended to have declining and elderly populations, with no work for young people, many of whom were forced to move away in search of employment; there were few services for the visitor. The blossoming of the RLS Trail, along with initiatives to promote forms of green tourism, has brought life back into these areas, with plenty of *gîtes*, hotels and restaurants to accommodate the traveller, and local businesses opportunities and employment.

In the late 1980s and early 1990s, when accommodation along many sections of the trail was still hard to come by, some very long day-stages were required, with several detours off-route to find a bed for the night, if wild camping was to be avoided. Today, a Stevenson Association exists (see Appendix 5 – most of the *gîtes*, hotels and campsites along the route are members), with coordinated accommodation and readily available, annually updated leaflets and booklets listing establishments along the trail. There are also several baggage-transfer services on offer for those who do not wish to carry more than a very light daysac, and for those rash enough, hiring a donkey for all or part of the trail could not be simpler. So with plenty accommodation of all types to choose from, the day-stages given in this revised edition are much more even in length, with no excessively long ones. For those wanting to walk either shorter or longer days, there is also much more scope to do so, and still find somewhere to spend the night without detouring off-route.

Plaque of RLS and Modestine in Saint-Jean-du-Gard (Stage 12)

Nowadays absolutely everyone in the region knows the story of the Scottish writer who, early one morning in the autumn of 1878, set out from the sleepy village of Le Monastier-sur-Gazeille, with a donkey as sole companion, to traverse the Velay and Cévennes to the small town of Saint-Jean-du-Gard in the south. Do follow in the footsteps of RLS and Modestine across this glorious countryside; it will be a journey that you will remember with joy for the rest of your life. Armed with this guidebook, you should have few difficulties, but many pleasures.

Alan Castle, 2007

INTRODUCTION

The Robert Louis Stevenson Trail is a linear long-distance walk through the Velay, Gévaudan and Cévennes regions of southern France. It follows closely, but not exactly, the route taken by the writer Robert Louis Stevenson (affectionately known as RLS), accompanied by his donkey, Modestine, during the autumn of 1878, and later recounted in his first successful book, *Travels with a Donkey in the Cévennes* (1879).

The trail meanders south for some 225km (140 miles), from Le Monastier-sur-Gazeille near Le Puy in the Velay, across the Cévennes mountains, to finish at Saint-Jean-du-Gard, west of Alès. In so doing, it crosses some of the most remote and finest country in rural France, and visits numerous towns and villages of historical importance, including Pradelles, Le Pont-de-Montvert and Florac. The latter sections of the trail pass through the land of the Camisards, an area ravaged by nearly 100 years of religious war between the local Protestants and their Catholic rulers.

Although the title of Stevenson's book suggests that the trail is wholly within the Cévennes, this is not in fact the case. The walk actually starts in the Velay, remaining there until Langogne, where it enters the ancient district of Gévaudan, bordering on Vivarais, the modern Ardèche. The Cévennes are not actually encountered until Mont Lozère, just under the halfway mark. The trail passes through three modern *départements*: the Haute-Loire until just before Langogne, Lozère for much of the remainder of the journey, and Gard for the last few kilometres into Saint-Jean-du-Gard. The Haute-Loire belongs to the Auvergne region, while Lozère and Gard form part of the region of Languedoc-Roussillon.

The RLS Trail ('Le Chemin de Stevenson' in French) follows footpaths, ancient drove roads (*drailles*), bridleways and a number of quiet roads. It is not a particularly demanding walk in either terrain or distance, fitting conveniently into a fortnight's holiday, allowing time for sightseeing if required at the beginning and end of the walk, as well as at a number of points in between. It is suitable as a first walking holiday for those with little or no experience of long-distance walking, although it would be wise to reach some level of fitness before setting out.

The second half of the walk in the Cévennes is noticeably more hilly

Crossing the Loire (Prologue)

than the first stages in the Velay and Gévaudan, but by then the wayfarer should be 'trail fit', taking the relatively modest ascents and descents in his or her stride. It is difficult to compare the 'grade' of this walk with any in the UK as the landscape is so totally different from any encountered in the British Isles, and there are also factors to consider such as the heat of a summer sun in these southerly latitudes. That being said, the RLS Trail can be likened in severity more to the South Downs Way than to the Pennine Way, but there the comparison ends!

An inspection of the route followed by Stevenson soon reveals that the writer did not take a direct line through these hills, his path wandering several times to the west and east on its journey south. There are a number of possible reasons for this meandering route.

Firstly, it seems likely that Stevenson was not the best of navigators, and furthermore that the maps he carried may not have been very reliable (they almost certainly did not show the new roads that were being built at the time). In addition, many of the people he encountered were unwilling or unable to direct him to his desired destination, and on at least one occasion (at Fouzillac/Fouzillic) he became hopelessly lost.

Secondly, his inquisitive, educated mind encouraged him to seek out places of interest some distance

Every available bit of land is used, Le Pont-de-Montvert (Stage 8)

from the natural line of the route. This was almost certainly the reason for the detour to the west on his first day, as he sought, but never found, volcanic Lac du Bouchet.

Thirdly, there were relatively few places on the journey where his and Modestine's food supplies could be restocked. This may well have been the reason for the lengthy loop to Florac, down the Tarn valley, and back up the valley of the Mimente.

Lastly, the philosophy of Stevenson must be remembered – he 'travelled not to go anywhere, but to go'.

Several of the paths and tracks used by RLS in 1878 have now been metalled and incorporated into the road network, which is why the trail

described in this guidebook does not follow exactly in the footsteps of Stevenson and Modestine. The modern route was designed to provide as scenic a walk as possible, avoiding busy roads and making use of France's excellent system of tracks and footpaths. Nevertheless, the itinerary described visits all of the principal towns and villages mentioned by RLS, with the exception of those in the Tarn valley between Le Pont-de-Montvert and Florac.

Stevenson entered the area at Le Puy-en-Velay, where he did much of the shopping for the innumerable items of gear that he took with him on his journey. The modern walker will also almost certainly arrive first at Le

Puy before continuing on to Le Monastier. As a preliminary to the RLS Trail, visitors are highly recommended to spend at least a day exploring Le Puy – a very attractive and historic town – and then either taking public transport to Le Monastier, as RLS did, or walking there.

For those who want to reach the start of the RLS Trail on foot, there is an excellent route, part of the GR430 (or 'Chemin de Saint-Régis'), from Le Puy, via Coubon on the River Loire, to Le Monastier-sur-Gazeille, and this is described in what I have called the Prologue, preceding Stage 1.

RLS had originally intended to walk all the way to Alès, but in the end, for various reasons, stopped his pedestrian journey at Saint-Jean-du-Gard and took a stagecoach on to Alès. For those who want to continue on foot from Saint-Jean-du-Gard to Alès, a walking route following sections of three other long-distance trails – the GR61, GR67 and GR44D – makes this possible, and is described in the Epilogue in this guidebook.

ROBERT LOUIS STEVENSON

Robert Louis Stevenson was born at 8 Howard Place in Edinburgh on 13 November 1850. The only child of Thomas and Margaret Stevenson, he was christened Robert Lewis Balfour Stevenson, and although the 'Lewis' was later changed to the French spelling, the pronunciation of the final 's' was retained all his life. It was this name, Louis, by which he was known to family and friends.

Stevenson was a sickly child whose schooling was often interrupted by chronic respiratory illnesses. In an attempt to alleviate the symptoms, he was sent to spend extended periods in the warmer parts of Europe, principally France, where he often stayed with his mother in Menton on the Côte d'Azur. An imaginative boy, he spent long periods alone as a child, developing a taste for literature and a desire to become a writer from an early age. His first attempts at writing were made at the age of 16.

From a family of eminent engineers, Stevenson's grandfather, Robert, was a celebrated civil engineer, while his father was appointed Inspector of Lighthouses in Scotland. Louis was expected to follow in his father's footsteps, and to this end was sent up to Edinburgh University in 1867 to read engineering. However, he had no interest in the subject and without qualifying he changed to study law, much to the bitter disappointment of his father. He eventually qualified as an advocate (the Scottish equivalent of a barrister), but never practised.

His desire to write continued into his young adult life, despite his father's belief that writing was not a suitable career. In 1873 he met Mrs Frances Sitwell, a beautiful and intellectual woman who became his confidante, introducing him to Sidney

*Carved wooden monument of Stevenson and Modestine,
Le Bouchet-Saint-Nicolas (Stage 2)*

Colvin, Slade Professor of Fine Art at Cambridge. Colvin was to remain a lifelong friend, critic and sponsor of RLS (see the dedication and letter to Sidney Colvin that act as a preface to *Travels with a Donkey*), and it was Colvin who helped Stevenson to get many of his early works published in literary magazines.

His meagre earnings from these early writings, together with small allowances from his father, enabled him to spend much of his mid-20s, the period between 1873 and 1879, in France. He became a 'bohemian' during this period, wearing his hair long and frequenting art colonies in and around Paris, a life he was introduced to by his cousin, a painter. In 1876 Stevenson undertook a short adventure with his friend Sir Walter Simpson, canoeing along the rivers and canals of France and Belgium. His exploits were later assembled into his first published book, *An Inland Voyage* (1878).

On his return to the art colony in Grez, Stevenson met and fell deeply in love with an American woman 10 years his senior, Mrs Frances (Fanny, or F) Matilda Osbourne, who was separated from her husband and living with her two children in Europe. In 1878 Fanny Osbourne returned to California in pursuit of a divorce, leaving Stevenson distraught in France. Partly to console himself for this temporary loss, and partly to provide material for a second book, RLS left for the Auvergne and Cévennes, an

18

area hitherto unknown to him. He was then 27 years old. After spending a month in Le Monastier, he set out on Sunday 22 September, accompanied by his newly acquired donkey, Modestine, on his now famous journey on foot through the Velay, Gévaudan and Cévennes.

Returning to Scotland, Stevenson adapted the journal he had kept while on the walk and presented it for publication as *Travels with a Donkey in the Cévennes*. It was published the following year, 1879, and was to become his first successful book. In the same year he followed Mrs Osbourne to California, where he spent the winter desperately short of money. Fanny eventually obtained a divorce, and on 19 May 1880 she and Stevenson, then 29 years of age, were married, and Fanny was to devote the next 14 years of her life to caring for a husband who was often ill.

In the same year as their marriage, Stevenson was diagnosed as suffering from tuberculosis. Nevertheless, the sunshine and warmth of California were beneficial to his health, and it was during this period that he was at his most prolific and successful as a writer, producing the classics *Treasure Island* (1883), *A Child's Garden of Verses* (1885), *Dr Jekyll and Mr Hyde* (1886) and *Kidnapped* (1886). Periods of calm and happiness were interspersed with bouts of illness, which he tried to relieve with trips to Switzerland, the south of France and Bournemouth.

Between 1887 and 1888 he stayed at Saranac Lake, New York State, where he was pronounced (wrongly) as cured.

In the search for new writing material, and on receipt of a huge advance from his publisher, Stevenson chartered a yacht to the South Pacific. Accompanied by Fanny, and his mother and stepson, they spent a year travelling, visiting Marquesas, Tahiti, Hawaii, Micronesia and Australia. After this period, in 1890, RLS bought a tropical estate of 400 acres on the island of Upolu in Western Samoa. Here at Vailima (Five Streams) he built a large house in which he entertained native dignitaries and visiting westerners. He settled down to a new life in a climate that was to his liking, becoming involved in local politics and writing some of his best works. He was part way through *The Weir of Hermiston* (published posthumously in 1896) when he died suddenly, shortly after a massive cerebral haemorrhage, on 3 December 1894. He is buried on the summit of Mount Pala, his famous 'Requiem' from *Underwoods* inscribed (incorrectly) on the tomb. The correct version is as follows:

'Here he lies where he longed to be;
Home is the sailor, home from sea,
And the hunter home from the hill.'

A visit to Western Samoa and to Vailima is highly recommended.

'TRAVELS WITH A DONKEY IN THE CÉVENNES'

Robert Louis Stevenson's journey through the Velay, Gévaudan and Cévennes began on Sunday 22 September 1878 and lasted for just 12 days, terminating at Saint-Jean-du-Gard on Thursday 3 October.

As a walking tour, it was relatively short and modest in nature, and hardly ranks highly amongst the long catalogue of adventurous journeys undertaken on foot by Victorian travellers. Nevertheless, *Travels with a*

Stone stèle *commemorating Stevenson's walk (Stage 1)*

'Travels with a Donkey!' A wayfarer with a heavily laden donkey on the RLS Trail near Saint-Germain de-Calberte

Donkey in the Cévennes, describing his adventures, is a delightful minor classic, still in print and much read today. The journey has captured the imagination of both walkers and lovers of literature alike ever since the publication of the book, and the route pursued by Stevenson through this ancient landscape in southern France is followed faithfully by many present-day ramblers. (Summaries of some of Stevenson's exploits on the trail are given in the various 'Travels with a Donkey' sections included in the stages of the route description, and details of his itinerary can be found in Appendix 3.)

RLS had resided in Le Monastier-sur-Gazeille for several weeks before embarking on his trek, and it was in this town that he purchased Modestine, the female donkey that was to accompany him on his travels. He must have aroused considerable curiosity amongst the local inhabitants, 'A traveller of my sort was a thing hitherto unheard of in that district.'

Certain writers and poets have been renowned for their walking prowess. For example, William Wordsworth was an ardent tramper of the English Lakeland fells and valleys – it has been estimated that during his long life he walked around 180,000 miles for pleasure. Hilaire Belloc and William Hazlitt were other well-known ramblers. However, RLS cannot be placed in this category; he undertook relatively few walking

View from the Cabane à Bonnal (Stage 9)

excursions, and in fact no other extended travels on foot are recorded after his sojourn in the Cévennes. Stevenson was primarily a writer, and the main reason for undertaking the Cévennes trip was to obtain material for publication.

Why Stevenson chose to tour the Cévennes without a human companion may have been partly because he wanted time to consider his entanglement with Fanny Osbourne, but more probably because he saw his task as a job of work, amassing information and experiences that he could convert into a book on his return home.

In an essay on the merits and pleasures of walking, written during this period of his life, Stevenson advised solitude on a walking tour, suggesting that only when alone can you fully appreciate the experience of being out in the countryside. (Solitary tramping is perhaps less popular today, and indeed some authorities frown on it from a safety point of view, although it was strongly advocated by that 20th-century guru of hill walking, Alfred Wainwright.)

The religious persecution of the Protestant Camisards by their rulers would have resonated strongly with Stevenson, who was well aware of the British established church's persecution of the Scottish Covenanters (a strict Protestant sect) in the 17th century. Middle-class Scottish Protestants would be much more likely to purchase a book that detailed a region of France that had a strong Protestant culture, rather than the predominantly Catholic remainder of France.

Needing time to write his daily journal was the main reason for several late daily starts. Of the 12 days on the trail, five were really only 'half-day' walks. Late starts sometimes resulted in his arriving at a destination in the dark, for example at Saint-Germain-de-Calberte, and on the last day in Saint-Jean-du-Gard.

The notebook compiled by RLS while on his Cévennes journey was rediscovered in the 1970s in the Huntingdon Library at San Marino, California, by an American relative of a Club Cévenol member. It was published in French by Club Cévenol, and in English in 1978 by Mainstream Publishing (Edinburgh), under the title *The Cévennes Journal* (see Appendix 4).

The aspect that distinguishes Stevenson's journey through the Cévennes from all other well-known accounts of pedestrian wanderings is the presence of the 'diminutive she-ass', Modestine. Not only does the donkey provide an admirable title for his subsequent book, but she also forms the central character of the tale, providing considerable literary copy. RLS probably did not have this in mind when he acquired the donkey, which he judged necessary for carrying the voluminous and heavy equipment he considered essential for camping out in the wild.

From a walker's point of view, to take a donkey on such a trip, particularly a female animal on heat, was a mistake, involving the expenditure of a great deal of nervous and physical energy on the part of Stevenson in persuading the animal to progress at a reasonable pace. But from a literary point of view, and this was how his adventure was later to be assessed, the inclusion of Modestine was a triumph. *Travels with a Donkey in the Cévennes* might well have suffered a very different fate had RLS chosen to journey completely alone. As it is, the book was his first real success, launching him on a career that was to produce some of the classics of the English language. (If Stevenson had not gone on to achieve such literary fame, it is a matter for conjecture whether *Travels with a Donkey* would be read so avidly today and the trail followed by so many modern pilgrims.)

Walking the RLS Trail today can be a rather eerie experience at times, almost like following in the footsteps of a ghost, and engendering a strong feeling of one's own mortality. In many ways, this quiet region of France is much the same today as it was in the 1870s, but the people Stevenson describes, children and all, have long since departed this life.

FIRST HALF OF THE TRAIL

The Massif Central – Velay, Gévaudan and Vivarais

The first half of the RLS Trail passes through the areas known as the Velay and Gévaudan, and skirts the ancient

View from Rocher de la Fagette (Stage 3)

region of Vivarais, the modern Ardèche. These regions, together with the Auvergne, and including the Cévennes, are all part of the Massif Central, the high mountainous plateau of southern-central France. This largely remote area of some 93,000km² (36,000 square miles) is a major source of hydroelectric power for France. The only major city in the region is Clermont-Ferrand (pop. 155,000), industrial in nature, situated to the north of the area covered by this guidebook. Much of the land in the Massif Central is above 1000m (3278ft), the highest point being the Puy de Sancy at 1885m (6180ft), above Le Mont-Dore to the southwest of Clermont-Ferrand. (The notorious mistral wind of the eastern Mediterranean originates in the cold air above the Massif Central.)

An old saying in this region of France is that the Auvergne is a 'gift of its volcanoes'. The landscape as seen today, with its many pointed *puys* and *sucs* (plugs or pinnacles of volcanic rock), is the product of vigorous volcanic activity over a vast period of time. Much of the land was shaped by gigantic earth movements around 35 million years ago, at the same time that the Alps were being formed by the African tectonic plate colliding with Europe. Many other volcanoes in the Auvergne are of much more recent origin – considerable volcanic activity took place in the area around 8000BC.

23

There are many thousands of extinct volcanoes in the Auvergne, often strung out across the landscape as chains of *puys*. The most well-known areas are the Puys de Dôme and Mont-Dore to the west and south-west of Clermont-Ferrand, Cantal to the west of Saint-Flour, and the Velay around its capital, Le Puy. This region of France holds many attractions for the walker, and further exploration on foot is highly recommended.

Le Puy is a very popular tourist centre, with much to offer the discerning visitor. The source of the Loire, one of France's most attractive and well-known rivers, is to be found in the Velay, on the slopes of Le Gerbier de Jonc (1551m/5085ft) to the south-west of Le Puy. The River Loire penetrates the heart of the Velay, giving its name to the modern *département* of the Haute-Loire. Near to Le Gerbier de Jonc is the watershed between the Atlantic and Mediterranean. Not far away lies Mont Mézenc, at 1753m (5747ft) the highest peak in the Velay, and seen in the distance in the early stages of the RLS Trail. The region can be more fully explored on foot by following the GR40, the circular Tour of the Velay (see Appendix 4).

At Langogne the Velay is left behind and the area known as Gévaudan entered. This remote, sparsely populated land, home of the legendary 18th-century Beast of Gévaudan (see Points of Interest, Stage 5), borders on another ancient region of France, the Vivarais. This little-known area dates back to before the French Revolution, to the time of the *ancien régime*. There are several GR trails throughout Vivarais, perhaps the most rewarding being the GR420 'Tour of the High-Vivarais', a circular route of some 201km (125 miles).

There are many *drailles* (or drove roads) in this part of France. These were used for centuries for moving animals from lower to upper pastures for the summer months, in the system known as transhumance. Several hundred sheep, with an ass or two and a few goats, would be herded up to the hills in April by two or three shepherds, and the shepherds would remain in the high pastures with the flock until the return to the lower valleys in September, October, or even November if the weather held. This system continued until the late 1970s, but nowadays most of the movement of stock takes place along the main roads in lorries. The traditional ways of this ancient land are fast disappearing with the 'progress' of the 21st century, but the *drailles* make excellent cross-country walking tracks, and several have been incorporated into the RLS Trail and other GR routes in the area.

SECOND HALF OF THE TRAIL

The Cévennes and the Parc National des Cévennes

The Cévennes is a rugged mountainous region forming the southeastern

Traditional Cévenol farmhouse

edge of the Massif Central. The northern boundary of the Cévennes is generally taken to be the high tableland of Mont Lozère, the summit of which, at 1699m (5570ft), is its highest point. The region extends southwards to Mont Aigoual (1565m/5130ft), a peak of granite and schist which, after Mont Lozère, is the best-known mountain in the area.

The Cévennes is bordered by the Vivarais and the depopulated Margeride in the north, the limestone causses to the south and west, and to the east lies Alès, the largest town in the region. It is a land of wooded hillsides, mountains and rushing streams, the many tributaries of the River Gardon forming deep, steep-sided valleys. The River Tarn rises in the Cévennes. It flows through Florac, then on for 354km (220 miles) to join the River Garonne, and is best known for the spectacular Tarn gorges found to the west of Florac.

The Protestant country of the Cévennes was witness to many atrocities during the Camisards' revolt in the 18th century (see Le Pont-de-Montvert – Stage 8). The modern-day Cévenols, although greatly depleted in numbers, are rightly proud of their fine, rugged landscape and their ancient traditions.

In the past the people lived largely on chestnuts (see Points of Interest, Stage 11), olives and vines, but today the population has a high percentage of elderly people, as many younger people have moved to towns in search of employment. Most Cévenols work on the land or in the tourist industry.

The Cévennes National Park, the second largest of the six national parks in France, covers an area of 91,416 hectares (225,889 acres). The park was created in 1970 to protect the landscape and curb the commercial exploitation of the region. There are restrictions on hunting and on the use of tents and caravans within the park boundaries. Planning permission is required for any new building, and for the renovation of old buildings, in an attempt to preserve the traditional styles of architecture characteristic of the region. Over 2200 plant species flourish in the park, which is proud to boast that although it occupies only 0.5% of the area of France, examples of around 50% of all the species of animals and plants that live in the country are found here.

For the walker there are some 1200km (c. 750 miles) of waymarked trails, GR, GR de Pays and PR routes, as well as many nature trails. The RLS Trail enters the park at Mont Lozère (Stage 8), and much of the remainder of the walk lies within its boundaries. Since 1984 Le Parc National des Cévennes has been twinned with Le Parc National du Saguenay in Quebec, Canada.

There is much to please the naturalist in the Velay and Cévennes. The woodland is a mixture of deciduous trees and conifers, with oak, beech and chestnut the predominant species. In the summer the air is often scented with honeysuckle and gorse. There is an abundance of wild flowers, particularly in spring. A large variety of wild mushrooms can be found, but great care should be exercised, as several are highly toxic. The area is rich in wildlife, animals and birds suffering relatively little from the activities of man. There are buzzards, kestrels and kites, and with luck even eagles may be spotted. Wild boar are said to roam the woods, but a sighting would be a rare occurrence. Even the most unobservant walker will be aware of the insect life, particularly the stridulation of cicadas during the hot summer months, the noise of which can be remarkably loud at times.

CLIMATE – WHEN TO GO

In general terms, summers in the Massif Central tend to be hot and relatively dry, while winters are often cold with heavy snowfalls.

In theory at least, the RLS Trail could be walked at any time of the year, although during the winter months very low temperatures coupled with snow and ice would call for considerable experience, particularly on the steeper sections on the southern half of the route. Moreover, hotel and other accommodation would probably pose quite a problem during winter, except in the skiing areas of the Cévennes. Most people, therefore,

Leaving Pradels (Stage 6)

would probably want to consider only spring, summer or autumn to walk the trail. Summer is undoubtedly the most popular season, although it does have some disadvantages. Firstly, it can become intensely hot during the day in July and August, and care must be taken to avoid sunstroke and dehydration. Secondly, finding accommodation for each night will be more of a problem in summer than in early or late season (see Accommodation, below).

The flowers and general freshness of springtime are recommended, but so is autumn, when the golden-brown tints of turning leaves can be particularly beautiful, chestnuts are everywhere on the ground, mushrooms of every size and hue abound in the forests, and the hedgerows are ripe with abundant fruits. However, temperatures can be quite low both early and late in the year, and there can be fairly dramatic changes in weather conditions – much of the trail lies at or above the 1000m (3278ft) contour, so it is not surprising that temperatures often drop rapidly. Remember that Stevenson experienced cold and unpleasant weather on the first part of his journey in late September (as did the present author in 2006!). Violent thunderstorms, often with little warning of their approach, are not uncommon at any time of the year, but particularly after the heat of a summer's afternoon.

TRAVELLING TO AND FROM THE RLS TRAIL

Travelling to the southeast of France from the UK couldn't be easier these days, with several budget airlines offering inexpensive flights to Nîmes, Montpellier, Saint-Étienne, Lyon and Clermont-Ferrand, from Luton, Stansted and Heathrow in the southeast, or Liverpool and Prestwick, amongst others, in the north. The arrival airport of choice is Nîmes, to where there are daily flights from several British airports. The bus timetable from Nîmes airport to the centre of Nîmes is such that it meets all of the major flights. The bus journey time from the airport to the centre of Nîmes is around 20–30 minutes, stopping at Nîmes railway station. Alternatively, there are always taxis available from the airport into the centre of town, which are not overly expensive over the modest distance.

From Nîmes it is about a five-hour train journey to Le Puy-en-Velay, usually with a change at Brioude or Saint-Georges-d'Aurac. An alternative would be a direct train from Nîmes to Langogne, and bus from there to Le Puy-en-Velay. For those wanting to start on foot from Le Monastier-sur-Gazeille, there is the choice of a somewhat infrequent bus service from Le Puy, or otherwise a taxi will not prove very expensive over the relatively short distance. Returning to Nîmes at the end of the trail takes around two hours on one of the fairly frequent buses from Saint-Jean-du-Gard via Mialet to

Alés, from where an excellent train service operates to Nîmes (journey time about 20 minutes). For further details of local train and bus services, see Public Transport in the Velay and Cévennes, below.

There are two other methods of reaching the area: train and long-distance coach. Train travel involves taking Eurostar (or train and ferry) from London to Paris, then a connecting train to Le Puy. On the return, book a train from Alés to Paris (the Nîmes to Paris main line) and back home on Eurostar. Long-distance coach services operate to the south of France from Victoria Coach Station in London.

There are three reasons why driving a private car to the Velay/ Cévennes in order to walk the trail is generally not advisable: it will undoubtedly be more expensive to drive than take a flight, train or coach (unless the car is filled with passengers); somewhere will have to be found to park the car safely for the duration of the walk; public transport will have to be used in any case to return to the start of the trail to retrieve the car.

PUBLIC TRANSPORT IN THE VELAY AND CÉVENNES

Trains

Timetable and booking information for French railways (SNCF) is easily obtained online (see Appendix 5). French railways are generally fast, clean and reliable, and offer good value for money. Prices of rail tickets tend to be reasonable (and not exorbitant when buying tickets from the railway station itself on the day of departure, as can be the case in Britain). Booking tickets in advance is advisable if travelling on French public holidays or during the main summer holiday period, but otherwise not usually essential for the journeys required to reach the RLS Trail.

Three main train lines pass through the region covered by the Stevenson Trail: the Nîmes to Paris main line, stopping at Alés, Génolhac, Villefort, La Bastide-Saint-Laurent and Langogne; the Le Puy-en-Velay to Saint-Étienne and Lyon line; the local La Bastide-Saint-Laurent to Mende line via Chasseradès.

If you are over 60 years of age, be sure to tell the person selling you the train ticket, as you are entitled to a significant reduction – usually 30% off the normal price of the ticket (you may be asked to show your passport). Also, remember that when travelling by train in France, you must validate your ticket by date stamping it before boarding the train. This simple task is performed using the orange-coloured machines (*composteurs*) located on the concourse of nearly every French railway station. (Failure to do so may result in a fine.)

Buses
Buses operate between many of the villages and towns along the trail, but the services are generally rather infrequent. Some of the services operate only once a day, and some even less frequently. A few services run only on school days, Monday to Friday, but not during school holidays. Winter timetables are generally inferior to summer, and usually start from early to mid September. The main bus routes of interest to the RLS Trail walker are Le Puy to Le Monastier (Cars Masson, tel 04.71.03.85.80), Le Puy to Langogne and on towards Mende (Cars Hugon Tourisme, tel 04.66.49.03.81), Florac to Cassagnes and on to Alès (Cars Reihes, tel 04.66.45.00.18) and Saint-Jean-du-Gard to Alès (Cars Fort, tel 04.66.85.30.28, Cars Lafont Tourism, tel 04.66.85.30.21, and Coopcar, tel 04.66.52.01.45, www.coopcar.fr).

Local tourist offices (see Appendix 5) will supply up-to-date timetables.

ACCOMMODATION

Hotels and *Gîtes d'étape*
These days, booking accommodation along the trail from the UK is relatively easy, thanks to the internet and e-mail. Many of the hotels and *gîtes d'étape* along the route now have websites, and enquiries and bookings are possible by e-mail. A list of accommodation specifically for the RLS Trail can be obtained from the Association Sur Le Chemin de Robert Louis Stevenson, making accommodation research particularly easy (the association's website is particularly

Inside Goudet's gîte d'étape (Stage 1)

recommended – see Appendix 5). Alternatively, main tourist offices in the region will send out lists of accommodation on request (again, see Appendix 5).

The RLS Trail is now very popular in France, and during the main summer season many of the establishments along the way will be fully booked, so if you intend to walk the trail during July and August, or over French public holidays, making reservations in advance is strongly advised (and May can also be a popular time for the French to walk the trail). At other times of the year, advance booking may not be necessary, although it is always advisable, if possible, to

phone for a booking at least one or two days ahead. If speaking French over the telephone is a problem for you, either ask the proprietor of your current hotel or gîte d'étape to phone ahead for you, or request the staff of a tourist office to do so.

Hotels in France are graded following a star system very similar to that used in Britain. A basic hotel is a one-star establishment, usually reasonably priced, clean and comfortable. Most of the hotels in the area covered by this guidebook carry a one- or two-star grading. Hotels are generally cheaper in France than in Britain. One pays for the room, so there is seldom a reduction for single occupancy, although if walking alone always ask for this.

The French *gîte d'étape* is similar to a UK youth hostel, but operated either privately or by the local community (*gîte communal*). There is no umbrella organisation to join, but details of all of them can be found on the www.gites-refuges.com website. *Gîtes d'étape* provide basic and inexpensive accommodation (generally considerably cheaper than British hostels) for the outdoor enthusiast, especially the walker, and many are in sympathetically restored traditional buildings. A typical *gîte d'étape* will accommodate between 10 and 30 people, and as in British hostels there is now a tendency for smaller dormitories, often with four, six or eight beds, and sometimes, but rarely, with two. The *gîte* will have a kitchen equipped with stoves and cooking utensils and there will be a dining area. There will be hot showers as well as washbasins and toilets. The warden or owner often does not reside in the *gîte d'étape*, but may live in an adjacent house or farm. Often, meals are provided by the guardian, and generally represent good value for money. (See Appendix 1 for a list of the *gîtes d'étape* along the RLS Trail.)

Camping

Official campsites are available for walkers to stay at most nights, and many of these offer special low rates for backbackers, and have restaurant and café facilities on site. Purists may wish to camp wild (*camping sauvage*) along the trail, 'à la Stevenson', but be aware that it is always necessary to seek permission first from the landowner. In addition, an uncontaminated water source will have to be located, unless sufficient water is carried from a town or village, and remember that wild camping is not allowed in the Cévennes National Park.

The art of the backpacker is to leave no sign of an overnight camp. Leave no litter and take care not to pollute water sources. Particular care should be exercised with matches and stoves, as forest fires are all too common during the hot, dry summers. Do not light open fires.

EQUIPMENT

The amount and type of equipment you take depends very much on whether you intend to use hotel and *gîte d'étape* accommodation, or camp out most (or all) nights. The most important consideration, always, is to ensure that your pack is as light as possible – do not take unnecessary items (RLS took an egg whisk!). Nothing more spoils a walking holiday than having to endure the excessive weight of an overloaded rucksac (unlike Stevenson, you will probably have no donkey to carry your pack). People who cannot resist taking a heavy rucksac are recommended to make use of one of the baggage-transfer services (see Appendix 5).

Beginning the descent from the Col de Saint-Pierre (Stage 12)

Parts of the trail along tracks and country lanes could be safely walked in a good pair of training shoes, particularly during the drier summer months. However, for the whole trail, and especially in the more rugged terrain of the Cévennes mountains, a pair of lightweight boots is recommended, preferably well worn-in. Lightweight shoes are also desirable for relaxing in the evenings, and for rest days and general sightseeing. (Boots may not be worn inside *gîtes d'étape*, and are discouraged inside most hotels.)

During the summer months this region of France usually experiences fairly high temperatures during the day, but at an average elevation of around 1000m (3278ft), it can become decidedly chilly once the sun has gone down. For much of the time shorts and a tee-shirt will be the most comfortable attire, but warm clothing should also be carried to allow for possible deterioration in the weather and for evenings. It is useful to pack a pair of lightweight walking trousers that can be worn on the occasional cold day or to protect sensitive skin against sunburn. Such trousers can also be worn in the evenings. Obviously, if walking during spring or autumn, more warm clothing will be required – Stevenson experienced some cold conditions on the first part of his journey in late September. A waterproof and windproof jacket is essential at any time of the year, and many people will wish to carry waterproof trousers.

The glare and heat from a southern summer sun can be intense, particularly during July and August, and a sunhat, high-factor suncream, lipsalve and sunglasses will all help to avoid over-exposure to the sun. To ensure that fluid is readily available during the day, at least one-litre bottle of water should be carried per person. The screw-cap plastic bottles in which mineral water is sold can serve as useful additional water carriers.

A rucksac is probably the most important item of gear needed, and its size will depend on whether or not camping equipment is to be carried. In heavy rain, a dustbin liner for the rucksac and a supply of plastic bags should keep the contents dry. Perishable food is best always kept in plastic bags to prevent accidental soiling of the inside of the rucksac. The camper will need to carry additional equipment, a small lightweight tent being the main requirement, plus a closed-cell type of insulating mat or a backpacking air bed, and a sleeping bag.

If you are going to cook your own food, the most convenient type of camping stove to use in France during the summer is one that burns gas. Spare gas canisters are readily available in France at campsites and village shops. (If travelling by air to France, remember that fuel cannot be taken on board an aircraft and will have to be purchased on arrival in

France.) A small cooking set and lightweight cutlery will also be needed, and don't forget a box of matches or lighter.

There are several miscellaneous items to consider. It is wise to include a small first-aid kit to treat any minor cuts and bruises, headaches or stomach upsets. Insect repellent may also be useful. A small torch may come in handy, and a mini French/English dictionary or phrasebook may help with communication. A Swiss Army knife, or similar, will provide a sharp blade for cutting (e.g. bread, salami), a pair of scissors, a can opener and a corkscrew (although remember not to pack it in your hand luggage when boarding an aircraft).

Modern-day travellers are advised to go **without** a donkey! It is in fact possible to hire donkeys for trekking in the Cévennes, and parties of walkers may well be seen leading (or not, as the case may be!) these pack animals. Having observed the antics of several such donkeys, and the exasperation of their masters, the author has concluded that the unwillingness and stubbornness of Modestine was not unique to that individual animal! If you must take a donkey, see Appendix 5 for donkey-hire firms in the Cévennes.

Last but not least, walkers may wish to take along a copy of Stevenson's *Travels with a Donkey in the Cévennes*, for to walk this trail is to make a literary and historical pilgrimage. However, the wayfarer is

33

Unloading the donkey at the end of the day (Stage 7)

advised to take also a guidebook (preferably this one!) and the relevant maps, plus a compass, for Stevenson leaves us in no doubt that he was a writer, not a geographer (as he was at pains to explain to Father Apollinaris at the Monastery of Our Lady of the Snows – see Stage 6). *Travels with a Donkey* is in no sense a guide to the trail, and it is sometimes a matter of conjecture as to the exact route taken by RLS. However, to refer while on the walk to Stevenson's accounts of various places along the way, and the people he encountered, will add much to the pleasure of this journey.

GRANDES RANDONNÉES

France has a very extensive network of official long-distance paths, called *grandes randonnées* (literally 'big walks'), and commonly abbreviated to GR. Each GR route has been designated a number e.g. GR7, GR65, etc. The principal long-distance trails usually carry a low number, e.g. GR4, GR6, whereas shorter circular routes, variations or links have two or three digit numbers. Trails in the vicinity of a one-digit GR route all carry the same first number. For example the GR4 has the associated GR43, GR44 and GR412; the GR6 has the associated GR60 and GR65, and so on. (This system is similar to the road-numbering system in Britain, e.g. M6, M62, M606, etc.) Note that circular GR routes are generally referred to as *tours*, e.g. 'Tour des Cévennes', the GR67.

There are at least 48,000km (30,000 miles) of GR trail throughout France, and the network is still expanding. The RLS Trail, 'Le Chemin de Stevenson', has been designated the GR70. In addition to the long-distance trails there are many usually shorter, regional footpaths, referred to as *GR de pays*, as well as an abundance of local footpaths or *sentiers de PR (petites randonnées)*.

WAYMARKING AND NAVIGATION

Like all other GR trails, the GR70 is waymarked with red-and-white paint stripes. These occur on rocks, boulders, trees, posts, fences, telegraph poles, and so on.

In 1978 a route for the RLS Trail was waymarked as part of the centenary celebrations of Stevenson's walk, and at that time the waymarking consisted of blue and blue-and-white stripes, as well as a number of blue-and-white wooden Saint Andrew's crosses. This waymarking is still encountered from time to time, but as the 1978 route was often different from the modern one, these old (often very faded) waymarks should not be followed. The Saint Andrew's crosses are now very rare along the trail, although in September 2006 there was still one in the main square in Pradelles (see Stages 3 and 4). As early as 1966–8 the trail between Le Monastier and Langogne was waymarked, with small metal signs showing the head of a donkey, by the Le Monastier scouts. Alas, only one of these signs remains today – at Courmarcès (see Stage 1).

In the GR waymarking system, various arrangements of red-and-white lines are used to signify different instructions. Two sets of red/white marks appearing together signify that a change in direction is imminent. This instruction is sometimes indicated by the use of curved red-and-white markings pointing towards the

Charming old but restored RLS Trail waymark (Stage 1)

Portail de la Verdette, Pradelles (Stage 3)

sometimes green or blue) paint stripes. Orange waymarks are for bridleways, sometimes occurring in the shape of a hoof print, signifying a horse or pony trail.

Certain notices should be understood. Both 'Propriété Privée' and 'Défense d'Entrer' mean that the area is private and entry forbidden. The signs 'Réserve du Chasse' and 'Chasse Privée' do not refer to

new direction to be taken. A painted cross, usually of one red and one white line, signals that the route is not in that direction – go back to pick up the correct trail. Remember also that all GR trails are waymarked with red-and-white flashes, so in areas where two GR routes meet, or where a variant leaves the main route, care should be taken to follow the correct GR trail.

Other waymarks will occasionally be seen. *GR de pays* are way-marked with red-and-yellow (e.g. Stage 6 to Notre-Dames-des-Neiges), whereas *sentiers de PR* are usually marked with single yellow (although

walkers, but indicate that hunting rights are reserved for the owner of the land.

However, extremely helpful as it is, the red-and-white waymarking of the RLS Trail should not be used as the sole means of navigation – the waymarks are only a guide indicating that the correct route is being followed. The sketch maps in this guidebook are not sufficient to follow the trail with accuracy either, and the relevant IGN maps (see below) should be purchased before setting out (and the ability to use a map in conjunction with a compass will be a distinct advantage). These maps will also be invaluable when detours from the main trail are taken, for example to visit a nearby place of interest, or to find lodgings for the night.

In sections where difficulties in following the route may be experienced, I have paid particular attention to the route description in this book. In a few areas where there could be confusion, I have given magnetic compass bearings – following these should solve problems if there is any doubt.

route. Some walkers, however, may find them adequate when combined with the route descriptions given in this guidebook and the waymarking. They are certainly ideal for the initial planning of the route at home.

If you wish to take some time off from walking the route to explore the Tarn gorges and the Causse Méjean near Florac, then IGN sheet 2640 OT at 1:25,000 is an essential purchase.

All of the above maps can be purchased from the specialist shops listed in Appendix 5.

MAPS

The recommended maps are IGN (Institut Géographique National, the French equivalent of the Ordnance Survey) maps at a scale of 1:25,000. These are high quality and provide considerable detail. Ten maps cover the whole of the route from Le Puy to Alès. The sheets required are, in order:

> 2735 E, 2736 E, 2836 O,
> 2737 E, 2738 E, 2738 O,
> 2739 OT, 2740 ET, 2740 E
> and 2840 O.

(E stands for est (east) and O for ouest (west).)

A much cheaper but less satisfactory alternative is to use IGN maps at 1:100,000 scale. Only two sheets are required – No. 50, Saint-Étienne/Le Puy (Le Monastier to Langogne) and No. 59, Privas/Alés (Langogne to Saint-Jean-du-Gard) – but they are far less useful than 1:25,000 maps for following an intricate crosscountry

SNAKES

The European viper or adder is not uncommon in the Massíf Central, and a bite, although unlikely to be fatal, would be exceedingly unpleasant, and could have serious consequences in the more sparsely populated regions through which the trail traverses, where help may not be quickly available. Fortunately they are fairly secretive animals, and likely to detect a walker's presence by vibrations along the ground and take avoiding action. Nevertheless, keep a good lookout for vipers in order to avoid accidentally treading on one. It is a good idea to familiarise yourself with the markings of the European viper (dark green/black in colour with characteristic zigzag stripes on the upper surface) in order to identify it, although the chances are that the trail will be completed without catching sight of one. A bite from a viper can

Fountain in Place de Mairie, Florac (Stage 9)

result in considerable bruising, discolouration, and swelling of the surrounding area. In the unlikely event that you are bitten, it is necessary to rest, avoid panicking, and get medical help as soon as possible.

EMERGENCIES

If you are unfortunate enough to require the assistance of any of the emergency services (medical help, police or fire brigade), these can be reached by dialling 112. This service is of course staffed by French speakers, and they are unlikely to speak much English. There is however an 'SOS Help' service in English, which can be contacted by dialling 01.4732.80.80. From a British mobile phone, dial 00.33.1.4732.80.80.

LANGUAGE

The French, like the British, are not particularly keen on learning foreign languages. Many of the younger people can speak some English, but in general do not expect the level of fluency found in Holland and Scandinavia. The Velay and Cévennes are sparsely populated regions where many of the villages and hamlets still have a preponderance of elderly people, who are able to understand only French. Some of the hotel and *gîte d'étape* proprietors are able to speak some English, but never rely on this. It is a good idea to brush up on 'rusty' French before the holiday – even the most elementary grasp of the language will pay dividends by enriching the experience of walking in France. However, no true adventurer will be discouraged by an inability to speak the local tongue, even if it necessitates the occasional use of sign language!

MONEY/BANKS/TELEPHONES

The unit of currency in France is the euro. Credit and debit cards are accepted widely, and as in Britain there are many ATM machines from which money can be withdrawn.

There are banks in Le Puy, Le Monastier-sur-Gazeille, Costaros, Landos, Pradelles, Langogne, Le Pont-de-Montvert, Florac, Saint-Germain-de-Calberte, Saint-Étienne-Vallée-Française and Saint-Jean-du-Gard. However, some of those in the smaller towns and villages are only open one or a few days a week, and then only for a few hours. The banks in the larger towns of Le Puy, Langogne, Florac, Saint-Jean-du-Gard and Alès operate normal banking hours. It is, nevertheless, advisable to carry from the outset sufficient currency for your needs.

Mobile phone coverage is variable, depending on the service provider and topography, although every village has a public phone box. However, it is now extremely rare to find a public phone in France that accepts coins, so if you intend to make use of public phones, it is a good idea to buy a French Telecom phonecard, easily available from most newsagents and general shops, at the start of the holiday.

INSURANCE

It is advisable to take out travel and medical insurance for the duration of the holiday. As most of the RLS Trail follows clear paths and tracks, it is unlikely that full 'mountain insurance' will be required, although it is best to ensure that the policy does cover the type of walking holiday you are going on. Certain rights are available for British subjects in France under reciprocal National Health Service arrangements within the EU, and it is a good idea to acquire a European Health Insurance Card, which is free. (For an EHIC application form and further information, either enquire at post offices in Britain, go to www.dh.gov.uk/travellers or telephone 0845 606 2030.)

PUBLIC HOLIDAYS AND TIME IN FRANCE

There are more public holidays in France than in Britain, although between June and October there are only two to consider – Bastille Day on 14 July and the Fête of the Assumption on 15 August. On both of these days the public transport system is affected and shops may be closed, although most cafés and restaurants stay open. In spring there are public holidays on 1 May (May Day), 8 May (1945 Armistice Day) and on Whit Monday. In autumn there are bank holidays on 1 November (All Saints' Day) and 11 November (1918 Armistice Day).

French time is one hour ahead of the time in Britain, i.e. French summer time is one hour ahead of BST and French winter time one hour ahead of GMT.

STEVENSON'S ROUTE BY CYCLE OR BY CAR

Although this guidebook is primarily intended for walkers wishing to follow Stevenson's journey on foot, it is perfectly possible to follow a similar itinerary on a bicycle or even by car. Indeed, as many of the tracks and paths used by RLS have now been incorporated into the modern road system, travelling by bicyle or car allows the actual route taken by Stevenson to be followed more exactly in certain areas, for example from Le Pont-de-Montvert to Florac, down the valley of the Tarn on the D998.

All the principal towns and villages visited by RLS can be reached using the road network, and much of the cycling or driving would be on pleasant, little-used D roads, where IGN maps at 1:100,000 are more than adequate. The information on facilities and places of interest given in this book will be of equal use to those travelling by bicycle or car as those on foot. Allow at least 2–3 days if travelling by car to allow time to search out the places visited by Stevenson. Cyclists will be able to use some of the tracks followed on the RLS Trail, but are advised not to attempt the whole route by bicycle.

CLUB CÉVENOL

Club Cévenol (see Appendix 5), founded in Florac in 1894 by a Protestant minister, Paul Arnal, is the

Houses perched precariously above the River Tarn at Le Pont-de-Montvert (Stage 8)

oldest and most active of the associations devoted to the Cévennes mountains and their inhabitants, and its interests also extend to the neighbouring limestone plateau of the Causses. The members of this non-profit-making organisation belong to a number of different groups, which include both resident Cévenols and *expatriates* living in Montpellier, Nîmes, Marseilles and Paris, as well as non-natives interested in the Cévennes and its future.

The objectives of Club Cévenol are threefold: to safeguard the natural and cultural heritage of the Cévennes and the Causses; to encourage the maintenance and creation of activities that will enable the inhabitants of the Cévennes and the Causses to stay in the land of their birth; to promote those forms of tourism which will preserve the special character of the area.

The club's journal, *Causses et Cévennes*, has appeared for over 100 years and is published quarterly. Club

Cévenol has also published a number of memoirs of notable figures in the history of the Cévennes, as well as a recording of Cévenol folk songs, sung by Jean-Noel Pelen in the ancient language of Occitan. However, the club is not only active in the cultural sphere, but also campaigns against inappropriate developments in the Cévennes, as well as promoting various types of green tourism, including walking the RLS and other trails in this most attractive region of southern France.

The commemoration in 1978 of the centenary of Stevenson's journey was due entirely to the efforts of Club Cévenol, and particularly the work and inspiration of Pat Valette, a Scottish woman who has lived in the Cévennes for many years. Also in 1978 the club published *RL Stevenson, Journal de Route en Cévennes* (a co-edition with Privat, Toulouse – see Appendix 4) to mark the centenary. This was prepared from the notebook used by RLS while in the Cévennes, which was discovered in the Huntingdon Library at San Marino in California by an American relative of a Club Cévenol member. Club Cévenol also organised several other events to coincide with the centenary, including waymarking parts of the RLS Trail and the special centenary walk of the route.

SUGGESTED ITINERARIES FOR WALKING THE RLS TRAIL

The standard itinerary described in this guidebook is designed to be completed within a fortnight by the average walker. The RLS Trail, from Le Monastier-sur-Gazeille to Saint-Jean-du-Gard, is broken down into 12 stages, each of which is intended as a day's walk. Time should be available at the beginning to fully explore Le Puy, and there is an optional day's walk from Le Puy to Le Monastier as a prologue to the start of the trip. A one- or two-day optional epilogue is provided at the end to relax in Saint-Jean-du-Gard, visit Mialet and the nearby Mas Soubeyran Camisard museum, and even, for the fit and experienced, to continue all the way on foot to Alès. More time will be needed if including all these options, and remember that severe weather can cause delay, so do bear this in mind when planning the length of your trip.

Those with more time available may wish to proceed at a more leisurely pace, visiting as many places of interest as possible on and a little off-route. Those with more limited time at their disposal, especially if they are fit walkers used to covering relatively long mileages each day, could cover the trial within about a week. Below are itineraries for both these 'leisurely' and 'fast' categories, making best use of the facilities available along the trail.

LEISURELY ITINERARY

A suggested itinerary for those with three weeks available who wish to enjoy the trail at a very leisurely pace and explore the area as much as possible.

Day 1	A day in Le Puy.
Day 2	Morning in Le Puy and afternoon walk to Coubon on the Loire.
Day 3	Coubon to Le Monastier-sur-Gazeille.
Day 4	Morning in Le Monastier-sur-Gazeille (visit museum). Afternoon walk to Goudet.
Day 5	Morning: Goudet to Le Bouchet-Saint-Nicolas. Afternoon: excursion to the Lac du Bouchet.
Day 6	Le Bouchet-Saint-Nicolas to Pradelles.
Day 7	Morning in Pradelles. Afternoon walk to Langogne.
Day 8	A couple of hours in Langogne and then walk to Cheylard-l'Évêque.
Day 9	Cheylard-l'Évêque to La Bastide (direct route on GR70 omitting the detour to the monastery of Notre-Dame-des-Neiges).
Day 10	La Bastide to the monastery of Notre-Dame-des-Neiges and return for a second night in La Bastide.
Day 11	La Bastide to Chasseradès.
Day 12	Chasseradès to Les Alpiers or Le Bleymard.
Day 13	Les Alpiers or Le Bleymard to Le Pont-de-Montvert.
Day 14	Le Pont-de-Montvert to Florac (this is the only long section that it is not easily possible to shorten, unless a 3.5km detour to the *gîte d'étape* at Mijavols is made, or a transport pick-up and drop-down the following day can be arranged, e.g. from the Col du Sapet). By taking the GR68 into Florac at the end of the day, a saving of nearly 4km of walking is made.
Day 15	Day in Florac with a possible excursion to the Tarn gorges.
Day 16	Florac to Cassagnas.
Day 17	Cassagnas to Saint-Germain-de-Calberte.
Day 18	Saint-Germain-de-Calberte to Saint-Étienne-Vallée-Française.
Day 19	Saint-Étienne-Vallée-Française to Saint-Jean-du-Gard.
Day 20	Day in Saint-Jean-du-Gard.
Day 21	Morning walk to Mialet with a visit to the Musée du Désert at Mas Soubeyran.

FAST ITINERARY

Below is a suggested itinerary for strong walkers with only 8 or 10 days at their disposal.

Day 1   Le Puy to Le Monastier-sur-Gazeille.

Day 2   Le Monastier-sur-Gazeille to Le Bouchet-Saint-Nicolas, with or without the optional excursion to the Lac du Bouchet.

Day 3   Le Bouchet-Saint-Nicolas to Langogne.

Day 4   Langogne to La Bastide-Puylaurent, omitting the detour to Notre-Dames-des-Neiges Monastery.

Day 5   La Bastide to Les Alpiers/Le Bleymard.

Day 6   Les Alpiers/Le Bleymard to Le-Pont-de-Montvert.

Day 7   Le-Pont-de-Montvert to Florac.

Day 8   Florac to Saint-Germain-de-Calberte.

Day 9   Saint-Germain-de-Calberte to Saint-Jean-du-Gard.

Day 10   Saint-Jean-du-Gard to Alès.

By omitting the first and last days, this itinerary allows the RLS Trail to be walked within eight days, but it is stressed that such a schedule is only possible by fit and experienced long-distance walkers.

HOW TO USE THIS GUIDEBOOK

Layout

The RLS Trail has been divided into 12 stages, each of suitable length for the average walker to complete within one day. Each stage terminates where some form of permanent overnight accommodation is available, usually a choice of hotels, *gîtes d'étape* and *chambres d'hôte*. In addition, there are prologue and epilogue sections. The Prologue contains details of Le Puy-en-Velay, a town that all RLS Trail walkers are recommended to explore before beginning the trail, and also includes a walking itinerary from Le Puy to Monastier-sur-Gazeille for walkers who wish to start their walk from Le Puy. The Epilogue provides details of relevant places to visit in and around Saint-Jean-du-Gard, at the end of the trail, and also describes a walking route from Saint-Jean to Alès for those who wish to finish their journey on foot, rather than take public transport to the city as did Stevenson.

Each stage begins with a 'summary table' showing the total distance for the stage, the distances between intermediate points, and an estimated

River Tarn looking back to the Pont de la Pontèse (Stage 9)

time to walk the section. Heights above sea level are given for the beginning and end of each stage, and for cols and peaks en route, but not at every location to avoid cluttering the tables and text. The summary table allows the basic details of the day's itinerary to be assimilated at a glance.

After the summary table a précis of the day's walk is given, followed by a section entitled 'Facilities', summarising the possibilities for finding refreshments and accommodation of all types along the way and at the end of the stage. This information will help those who wish to shorten or lengthen the day's walk to find somewhere to spend the night that is not at the 'recommended' end of the stage. Details of other facilities, such as banks, post and tourist offices are also included here. Remember that establishments can cease to trade, while others will open, so it is strongly suggested that an up-to-date list of accommodation

and other facilities along the RLS Trail is acquired just before leaving for France, or on first arrival in the area. This can be obtained either from local tourist offices or the Association Sur Le Chemin de Robert Louis Stevenson (see Appendix 5).

The 'Travels with a Donkey' section outlines the adventures of Stevenson and Modestine on each particular stage of the journey. The places visited by RLS, the people encountered, as well as Stevenson's deeds and thoughts, are summarised here, giving an overview of his journey. Part of the fascination of this walk is to compare one's own trip with that of Stevenson's journey, and identify the sights he saw and places he visited. Reading this section before walking each stage, in conjunction with the relevant pages of *Travels with a Donkey in the Cévennes*, will remind the walker of the events on Stevenson's original excursion. The

45

various RLS quotations are taken mainly from *Travels with a Donkey* in the Cévennes, but occasionally from his original journal, as published in *The Cévennes Journal*. All Stevenson quotes appear in blue type.

The next section is a detailed route description of the trail. When used in conjunction with the relevant IGN map, the walker should experience little difficulty in following the way. Special attention has been paid to those areas where route finding may be a problem or where the waymarking is particularly poor. Where alternative routes are possible, details of these are also given.

The final section has the title 'Points of Interest'. The main items of interest on or near the trail are all summarised and described here, and are followed by an ⓘ in the route description, for ease of reference. Background information is included to encourage an understanding of the culture and tumultuous history of the region, and to explain features of the landscape. In fact referring to this section before setting out each day should avoid the possibility of forgetting or missing an important monument, building or view. Details of longer excursions with sightseeing options on a rest day or 'day off' are also given for certain areas.

Distances and Altitudes

Distances in the 'Route' sections are given only in metres and kilometres, as IGN maps are metric, and to quote imperial units as well would be tedious and clutter the text and tables with too many conversions. Any readers unfamiliar with metric units of distance are reminded that a metre is just a little over a yard, and that to convert kilometres to miles divide by 1.6 (approximately). Main summits and cols are given in both metres and feet, but the majority of other heights in metres only, again so as not to clutter the text. A very approximate conversion of 1000m is about 3300ft. When the word 'metres' appears in the text this refers to linear distance, whereas 'm' after a number designates altitude in metres.

Timings

Times as well as distances are given for the various stages. These times are those that the 'average' rambler would be expected to maintain, but no allowance has been made for stopping to rest and/or admire the scenery, have lunch, and so on, which need to be considered when estimating the time required for the day's activities. These timings obviously take account of the distance, but even more importantly, they allow for the roughness or otherwise of the terrain, the steepness of paths and tracks, and amount of ascent and descent. The actual time taken will obviously vary from individual to individual, and depend on the prevailing conditions, but it is nevertheless useful to have an indication of the time generally required to walk a section. (The system is widely used in continental Europe.)

Tour Donjon and the White Madonna, Château de Luc (Stage 6)

PROLOGUE
Part 1 – Le Puy-en-Velay

The great majority of walkers embarking on the RLS Trail will enter the Massif Central region at Le Puy, but rather than making straight for the start of the trail at Le Monastier, consider relaxing and unwinding first by exploring this picturesque and unique French town. A full day is recommended if time is available.

Le Puy-en-Velay, with a population of around 27,000, is the *préfecture* of the *département* of the Haute-Loire. Situated on the River Loire, it is distinguished by a number of *puys*, or pinnacles of rock, volcanic in origin, on which are perched some of the town's best-known monuments. The highly photogenic 10th-century Romanesque chapel of Saint Michel de L'Aiguille ('Saint Michael of the Needle') is dramatically situated on the summit of the 80m high Rocher Saint Michel. A series of steps leads to the top.

The highest *puy*, at 757m (2482ft) above sea level, is the Rocher Corneille, on which stands the most famous landmark of Le Puy, the 112,000kg red statue of the Notre-Dame-de-France with the infant Jesus. This enormous statue, which is visible from most parts of the city, was made in 1860 from the metal of 213 melted-down cannons captured from the Russians at Sebastopol during the Crimean War. It stands 27 metres high and it is possible to climb up inside the hollow structure.

The 12th-century Romanesque cathedral stands half on the natural rock and half on pillars built into the hillside of Mont Anis. The influence of Moorish Spain and the east is seen in its Arabic and Byzantine features – the facade is particularly striking. Inside will be found a statue that is one of the few surviving 'Black Madonnas of the Auvergne'. The abbey cloisters are worth a visit, and the museum contains several fine frescoes, including one of the Crucifixion.

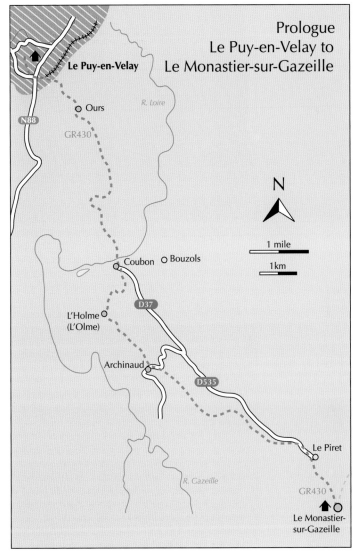

Prologue
Le Puy-en-Velay to
Le Monastier-sur-Gazeille

Festival craftsmen,
Le Puy

The old centre of the town is a maze of narrow streets dotted with lace-makers' workshops, and well worth an hour or two's exploration. A small tourist train ('Le Petit Train Touristique') operates during July and August, taking visitors around the tiny streets and up to the cathedral. Guided walks around the town and along the local GR and PR footpaths are also organised during the summer season (these of course are given in French). Ask at the tourist office for details.

Le Puy is host to a number of festivals during the summer. The Brotherhood of White Penitents, a Catholic order that originally cared for the sick, was established in Le Puy in 1584. They hold a spectacular procession in the town every 15 August, on the Feast of the Assumption.

Le Puy is also one of the four traditional starting points in France for the pilgrimage to the shrine of Saint James at Santiago de Compostela in northwest Spain (the others being Paris, Vézelay and Arles). The modern long-distance footpath, the GR65, follows a route of some 805km (500 miles) across France to enter Spain at Roncesvalles in the Pyrenees (see *The Way of Saint James – Vol 1: Le Puy to the Pyrenees*, and *Vol 2: The Pyrenees to Finisterre* by Alison Raju, Cicerone Press). A

further 644km (400 miles) or so along the northern edge of the Iberian peninsula leads to Santiago. The first steps on this mammoth trail are out of Le Puy on the Rue Jacques and the Rue de Compostela.

View of the old town of Le Puy

FACILITIES

Le Puy possesses a large number of one-, two- and three-star hotels. There is also a youth hostel, two *gîtes d'étape*, and a campsite (three star) is situated about 5km out of the centre of the town. There is ample choice of cafés, bars and restaurants, from the simplest snack to haute cuisine. As the principal town in the whole area, Le Puy has a wide variety of shops and many banks. Large numbers of tourists are attracted to the town, which specialises in lace making by hand, and lace shops abound. (Although expensive, lace is unbreakable and light to carry, and so suitable for walkers seeking presents for family and friends, even at the start of the holiday.) There is a large central tourist office where free maps of the town are usually available, as well as hotel and public transport information.

Part 2 – Le Puy-en-Velay to Le Monastier-sur-Gazeille

19.1km (11.9 miles)
5hrs 15mins

Location	Distance (km)		Time (hr. min)	
	Section	Cum	Section	Cum
Le Puy-en-Velay (625m)	0.0	0.0	0 00	0 00
Ours	2.3	2.3	0 45	0 45
Volhac	5.0	7.3	1 25	2 10
Coubon (633m)	0.5	7.8	0 05	2 15
L'Holme[1]	1.9	9.7	0 35	2 50
D 37 (Archinaud and Truchet)	2.0	11.7	0 30	3 20
L'Herm	4.2	15.9	1 05	4 25
Le Monastier-sur-Gazeille (930m)	3.2	19.1	0 50	5 15

[1](also spelled 'L'Olme' on some maps and signposts)

In many respects Le Puy is a more fitting starting point for the walk south than the smaller and less significant Le Monastier. The first dozen kilometres of a relatively new GR trail, the GR430, or 'Le Chemin de Saint-Régis', make an excellent introduction to the area, with the pleasant village of Coubon on the young River Loire as a halfway point, where those who make a late start from Le Puy may find accommodation and food.

ROUTE

The route begins in the heart of the old town of **Le Puy**, near to the cathedral. Walk along the cobbled streets to locate Rue Cardinal de Polignac. Walk west along this to the Rue Rochetaillade, where you turn left down cobbled steps to the junction of the Rue du Bouillon and the Rue de la Saulnerie. Here take the passageway ahead which bends to the left to reach Rue Meymard. Turn right down more cobbled steps on this narrow street to reach a square. Turn left here along the Rue Collège to reach

the official start of the GR430, at a sign indicating 'Circuit Pédestre de Saint Jean François Régis', opposite the Chapelle du Collège des Jesuites du Puy-en-Velay.

Turn right down cobbled Rue Bessat, and by so doing you leave the old town behind. Continue ahead at the Rue Chaussade to follow Rue Crozatier to reach wide and busy Boulevard Maréchal-Fayolle. Turn left along this but only for about 60 metres, to bear right onto Avenue Georges-Clémenceau. Cross the river Le Dolaizon followed by the main road, to climb up the Rue Pierre-Fairgoule opposite.

On reaching the Boulevard Phillipe-Jourde (railway station down to the left) walk along it for a few metres to take a right turn onto l'Avenue d'Ours-Mons, so at last climbing out of Le Puy. (Note that if coming directly from the railway station, without first visiting Le Puy town, then turn left out of the station, and in a few metres left again on the Rue Norbert-Rousseau, to reach in 100 metres the Boulevard Phillipe-Jourde and follow the route description from there).

Walkers at the beginning of the route leaving Le Puy

Climb on l'Avenue d'Ours-Mons to reach Rue Edouard-Estaunie where you turn right. This road soon bends sharply to the right to reach Espace-Municipal Bel-Air at a fire hydrant. Turn sharp left here up this sur-faced track, passing two benches. The trail soon becomes a grassy and cobbled track. Climb, ignoring any side turnings, to reach the outskirts of the village of **Ours**. ◄ Continue on the track, which soon gains a hard surface (Chemin de Bel-Air) and leads to the main road in this picturesque village, opposite another cruci-fix, this one dated 1932.

Pass a beautiful old stone crucifix, dated 1600, perched on a left-hand wall.

Cross the main road to descend half-right on the Chemin du Vallon. Be sure to look back during this descent to see the Château d'Ours. The lane bears to the left (east) at the old communal water fountain (non-drinking water). When the road swings sharply left again leave it to take an earthen track to the right. In 150 metres at a Y-junction take the right fork. This ancient, partly cobbled track climbs between drystone walls. ◄

Near the top look back to admire the view of the sur-rounding hills, with Le Puy spread-eagled below, the first view of open Auvergne countryside.

Continue to a road at a double bend in the latter. Keep ahead on this road for about 50 metres to where the road bends sharply left, and here continue ahead on an earthen track with views of tree-covered volcanic *puys* in the distance. Where the main track swings to the left, walk ahead on a narrow enclosed footpath between hedgerows, to emerge at a cross-tracks; maintain direc-tion (160 degrees magnetic). On reaching high-tension electricity cables at a large metal pylon, bear right on the track that veers to the left (trees on left and open field to the right). The track becomes tarmacked and passes a group of pines known as the 'Pins du Boulanger'. There are extensive views hereabouts: the once fortified castle seen ahead is in the small village of Bouzols on the far side of the Loire.

A few metres after the pine trees, turn right on a wide earthen track, heading westwards. Continue on this track to reach the edge of a surfaced road, by buildings and a GR3 sign on a concrete electricity pole. Turn left onto a gravel track to follow it southeastwards on the side of wooded Mont Jonnet, heading towards Coubon,

First cross on the trail, at Ours

seen in the valley below. Descend on the track to pass, on your right, a stone crucifix that carries a small body of Christ. Emerge from the trees to reach the small village of Les Esclos.

Descend on the road through the village to reach the D38. Turn left along it for about 50 metres to turn sharp left off this main road onto a minor road signposted to Le Chier. In a further 50 metres turn right down Rue Cesar-Franck. Continue ahead on the descent on the Montée des Mourges to reach the D37 at **Volhac**. Turn right and in a few metres turn left over the wide bridge over the River Loire to enter the pleasant village of **Coubon**, which sits on the banks of the river (water fountain here).

There are two hotels in the village as well as restaurants, bar and shops, but those requiring the campsite for

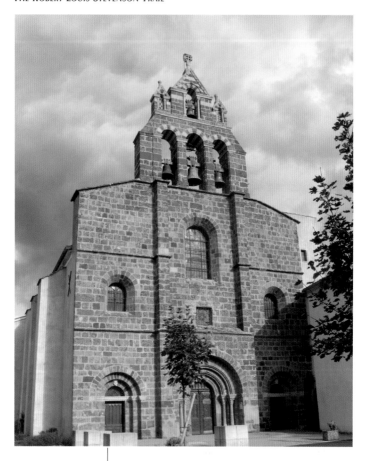

Parish church in Coubon

Backpackers enjoy a special low rate for camping overnight.

overnight accommodation should turn right along the south bank of the river for about 800 metres (ignore other signs to the campsite, which are for a much longer road route intended for motorists). The campsite is equipped with a bar/restaurant so there is no need for campers to retrace their steps into the village to find food and drink in the evening. ◀

Flower cart at L'Holme

After crossing the bridge over the Loire remain on the D37 for about 200 metres to where it bends to the left. Here bear right, signposted to L'Holme and La Roche (L'Holme is also spelled l'Olme). Follow the Route de l'Olme uphill. Where the road levels at an old cross (Croix de Petalou) follow the road round to the right (i.e. ignore the road straight ahead) still following the signpost for L'Olme and La Roche, climbing again. About 200 metres later ignore the right branch to La Roche, but remain on the road signposted to L'Olme and Poinsac. Just before the road levels again, pass another small stone cross on the left. Alas the ascent continues, but eventually the hamlet of **L'Holme** is encountered at yet another stone wayfarer's cross.

In the centre of this old hamlet locate a concrete electricity pole indicating where three GR routes separate. The GR3 goes ahead, but we turn left on the GR430 and GR70. This road leaves the hamlet and soon becomes a poorly surfaced track that climbs gently. On reaching a large building, pass to its left to descend gradually towards the buildings of **Archinaud** and Truchet to meet the D37. Cross this road and follow the minor road signposted to Bois Royer. Continue ahead at the buildings of the hamlet of Bois-Rouillier. Later ignore a track off to the right, remaining ahead through the Bois des Gondous. Later still pass a wide track at locked gates and a *'Chantier interdit au public'* sign, to follow the wide path ahead towards the trees, a pleasant route that leads to the hamlet of **L'Herm** (water fountain here).

Walk ahead to where the surfaced track swings to the left at the end of the hamlet; here walk ahead on a grassy track. This leads eventually to the D38. Turn right on this road to follow it towards Le Monastier, which soon comes into view ahead. Follow the D38 for about a kilometre to reach a road junction with the D27. Follow the latter ahead, signposted to **Le Monastier**, Centre Ville. Pass a stone crucifix on your left, and then a cemetery to follow the D49 into the village, along the Avenue du Puy, to reach and follow Rue Langlade on which is situated the village *gîte d'étape* (Emmanuel Falgon).

In the centre of the village, turn left following the sign for the 'Centre Historique'. The church is then in front of you. Here we part company with the GR430, which turns to the left. For an interesting short detour to visit the old town, turn to the right at the Place de L'Abbatiale. Pass a water fountain and walk up the street. At the back of the church you will find the *mairie* and opposite is situated the Musée Municipal Monastier, which among other exhibits has one on the life of Robert Louis Stevenson. After a visit here return to the high street to start the GR70 by walking southeast along the Rue Saint-Pierre to reach the Place de la Poste.

STAGE 1 – *Le Monastier-sur-Gazeille to Goudet*

10.2km (6.3 miles)
3hrs

Location	Distance (km)		Time (hr min)	
	Section	Cum	Section	Cum
Le Monastier-sur-Gazeille (930m)	0.0	0.0	0 00	0 00
Courmarcès	4.2	4.2	1 10	1 10
Le Cros	1.8	6.0	0 25	1 35
Saint-Martin-de-Fugères	1.7	7.7	0 25	2 00
Goudet (760m)	2.5	10.2	1 00	3 00

The RLS Trail begins by heading southwest from Le Monastier, following a series of rural tracks and footpaths, to pass through the hamlets and small villages of Courmarcès, Le Cros and Saint-Martin-de-Fugères, before a dramatic descent into the valley of the Loire to reach Goudet, above which is perched the picturesque Château de Beaufort.

FACILITIES

Le Monastier has two *gîtes d'étape*, a *chambre d'hôte*, a couple of hotel/restaurants, and a campsite located alongside the RLS Trail less than a kilometre from the village. There are three supermarkets in the village, two *boulangeries*, a *pâtisserie*, two banks with ATM facilities and a post office.

At Goudet there is an excellent *gîte d'étape*, the Hôtel-Restaurant de la Loire and a campsite down by the river. The latter has a café and an *épicerie* which is open to both campers and non-campers when the campsite is open during the summer season. Kayaks for use on the river can be hired from the campsite. The village café, the Café du Pont de la Loire, is on the far side of the road bridge over the River Loire.

TRAVELS WITH A DONKEY

'The best that we find in our travels is an honest friend. He is fortunate who finds many.'

Stevenson 'spent about a month of fine days' in Le Monastier before setting out on his travels. During this time he made several visits to Le Puy to purchase a huge bespoke sleeping sack, which would 'serve a double purpose – a bed by night, a portmanteau by day'. He gathered together a large and odd assortment of kit, including a revolver, jackknife, spirit lamp, pan, lantern, candles, books and an egg whisk. His provisions consisted of a leg of cold mutton, a bottle of Beaujolais, chocolate cakes and tins of Bologna sausages. To carry all this he acquired, for '65 francs and a glass of brandy', a donkey, 'a diminutive she-ass, not much bigger than a dog, the colour of a mouse, with a kindly eye and a determined under jaw'. The animal was immediately christened Modestine.

Storm clouds gathering over Le Monastier

The pair set out at 9am on Sunday 22 September 1878, Stevenson having spent several hours since he rose, just after 5am, attempting to load up the donkey. The first day was not a success. The pace set by the donkey was frustratingly slow for Stevenson, 'it was something as much slower than a walk as a walk is slower than a run; it kept me hanging on each foot for an incredible length of time'. He soon took to beating the animal with a stick and in this way reached Goudet, where the rocky grandeur of the scene impressed him. He stopped to sketch the Loire and Château Beaufort and had lunch at the inn, where he was shown a portrait of the landlord's nephew, 'Professor of Fencing and Champion of the Two Americas', which is still in existence today.

ROUTE

In **Monastier**'s ⓘ Place de la Poste, where the **Stevenson Plaque** (or *stèle*) is situated, a short stretch of road has been renamed Esplanade Stevenson, as it was from this very place that RLS stepped out on his journey south to Saint-Jean-du-Gard. Nearby is the Church of Saint Jean (water fountain outside), which is worth a visit before leaving the village. Admire the view down the valley from here before making the first strides on your pilgrimage through the Velay and Cévennes

From the 'Depart Stevenson' sign, walk along the Rue Saint-Jean for another 50 metres to the Place Saint Jean, from where you take the Rue Henri-Debard down to the right, passing the church. Descend into the valley below, passing a large, ugly *village de vacances* and housing estate (which was neither here in 1878, nor even in 1988, when I first strode this way). Ignore all side turnings to pass a campsite and cross the river by a bridge.

Pass a hotel/restaurant on your left (Le Moulin de Savin) to walk uphill on a well-defined track. The trail climbs steeply through woodland. Follow red-and-white and yellow waymarks, later ignoring a path descending to the right. On reaching the high point of the track

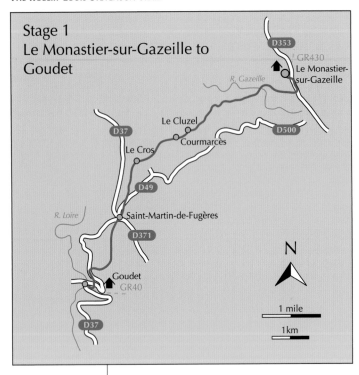

Stage 1
Le Monastier-sur-Gazeille to Goudet

(993m), now out of the woods, the main track swings to the left (the old route of the RLS Trail), but leave the main track here (waymarks on a solitary tree) to bear to the right downhill on a grassy enclosed track. This becomes sandy and climbs again.

On reaching the hamlet of **Le Cluzel** cross the small road bridge and then walk uphill on the minor road, with the buildings of Le Cluzel over to the right. Pass a restored (2003) communal washing area (fountain and series of water tanks) and continue ahead. Pass a wayside shrine and walk uphill to pass other buildings. At an ancient wayside cross perched on a small boulder at a crossroads, continue ahead on a surfaced track with buildings on your left. Soon pass on your left one of the original RLS Trail waymarks, which shows a donkey's head and the way to Saint Martin in 45 minutes. ▶

A few metres after the 'donkey' sign, where the gravel track ends, turn half-right across grass for 15 metres to turn left on a sandy track. This is an excellent, clear red earthen track through open pastures, with wide distant views. After a while ignore another path leading off to the right, but instead descend to cross a small river (Ruisseau du Cros) and climb to the village of **Le Cros**. After a few metres turn right at a concrete telegraph pole and descend and re-ascend on a marked track to a metalled road at a wooden telegraph pole.

Turn right onto the road, but in about 100 metres turn left to follow a clear track for about 1.2km to the D49. Turn right on this road, but in 60 metres, about 50 metres before the road sign indicating Saint-Martin-de-Fugères, turn left off the road onto a narrow path between hedgerows. Continue on a grassy path that soon swings right to enter **Saint-Martin-de-Fugères**. ⓘ

This metal signpost (see photo page 35), the only one of its type to survive, has been lovingly restored by the residents of this tiny village of **Courmarcès**. There is also a picnic table here, a good place for 'elevenses'.

Shrine at Le Cluzel

Home-made RLS Trail signpost in Saint-Martin-de-Fugères

From here there is an excellent view down to Goudet, the River Loire and the Château de Beaufort ('...opposite upon a rocky steep...'), the latter sketched by RLS.

Turn right at the war memorial, pass some public toilets, and then bear left downhill to pass the impressive west door of the village church. Join the D49, but after about 80 metres, just before the road sign indicating the limit of Saint-Martin-de-Fugères, turn left onto a dirt track, with a stone wall on your left. After about 250 metres, where the trail splits into three tracks, it is important that you take the middle of these three tracks, heading left, with a wall on your left and pasture to the right.

After about a kilometre this track descends to a farmhouse (Ferme de Prémajoux). Turn right at the end of a large barn, downhill on a grassy track between low drystone walls and later between barbed-wire fences. There follows a steep descent to the Loire valley on an obvious but somewhat eroded track. After a while be sure to bear right as indicated by a red-and-white waymark, keeping a wire fence on your right. At the next path junction bear right, still downhill. ◄

Descend to the main road, the D49, cross it and take the path that descends to the first houses of **Goudet**. ⓘ Descend steeply down to the village. Turn right at the *mairie*, following the sign, which indicates the Chemin de Stevenson. Reach and pass a hotel/restaurant (Hôtel de la Loire). The *gîte d'étape* is by the road bridge on the bank of the River Loire, opposite the telephone kiosk. The *gîte* is a converted barn –enquire first at the farmhouse. Campers will find the campsite on the bank of the Loire, reached by first crossing the road bridge over the river.

Morning view of the ruins of the Château de Beaufort above Goudet

POINTS OF INTEREST

Le Monastier

The Monastier Musée Municipal has, amongst other exhibits, one called 'The Life of Robert Louis Stevenson'. It is open during the summer (from 1 June to 31 October) from 10.30am to noon and from 2.30pm to 5pm, every day except Monday. The museum is housed in the château, which dates from 1525. The latter is constructed of basalt rock and has solid round towers topped with red-tiled roofs

The Stevenson Plaque (or *stèle*) commemorating RLS's journey (see photo page 19) is located under a tree outside the post office. It reads 'D'ici partit le 22 Septembre 1878 Robert Louis Stevenson pour son voyage à travers Les Cévennes avec un ane.'

Descending the old track into Goudet

The 11th-century abbey church of Saint Chaffre contains ecclesiastical treasure.

The River Gazeille is a tributary of the Loire.

The views of the twin *sucs* of Mont Breysse were sketched by RLS during his stay in Le Monastier.

Saint-Martin-de-Fugères

The church has an interesting seven-ribbed stone surround to the west door.

Goudet

Many of the old buildings of the village, including the *gîte d'étape*, were built from the stones of the Château de Beaufort, which was destroyed after the revolution of 1789. The ruins of the château, romantically situated on a rock above the Loire, make a most impressive sight in this deeply cut valley. Stevenson made a sketch of the scene. The early morning is the best time for a photograph, as the sun sets to the rear of the château producing a rather eerie silhouette. The château was in the process of restoration during 2006, but it is open for visits from 1 July to 1 September, daily from 10am to 7pm, with an entrance fee.

Note that the road bridge over the River Loire in Goudet is of modern design, but utilises one of the piers of an older bridge.

Arlempdes

About 2.4km south of Goudet, Arlempdes is another attractive village overlooking the Loire valley, with a castle perched on a rock above the river, and worth a visit if time is available.

STAGE 2 – Goudet to Le Bouchet-Saint-Nicolas

12.8km (8 miles), 3hrs 40mins

Excursion to Lac du Bouchet
10km (6.2 miles), 2hrs 45mins

Location	Distance (km)		Time (hr min)	
	Section	Cum	Section	Cum
Goudet (760m)	0.0	0.0	0 00	0 00
Montagnac	2.0	2.0	0 50	0 50
Ussel	2.5	4.5	0 45	1 35
Bargettes	3.1	7.6	0 50	2 25
Preyssac	2.6	10.2	0 40	3 05
Le Bouchet-Saint-Nicolas (1218m)	2.6	12.8	0 35	3 40
Excursion to Lac du Bouchet (restaurant)	3.4	3.4	1 00	1 00
D33	1.8	5.2	0 30	1 30
Le Bouchet-Saint-Nicolas (1218m)	4.8	10.0	1 15	2 45

After a visit to the ruins of the Château de Beaufort a stiff climb out of the Loire valley leads to the first of several small villages and hamlets on this gentle walk to Le Bouchet-Saint-Nicolas, which now boasts a fine wooden sculpture of Stevenson and Modestine. There is plenty of time for an afternoon excursion to Lac du Bouchet, the volcanic lake that eluded Stevenson.

FACILITIES

A café/restaurant will be found in Ussel, but otherwise do not expect any facilities en route until reaching Le Bouchet-Saint-Nicolas. Accommodation, cafés, a restaurant, shops, a post office and a bank can be sought at Costaros, a small town a couple of kilometres off-route, north from Bargettes. Note that one of the specialities of the region, *Le Puy lentilles* (lentils), can be bought from some of the farms passed en route today and from other outlets in the Le Puy region.

The old inn in Le Bouchet-Saint-Nicolas is the Auberge de Couvige in the centre of the village. Note that the *auberge* may be closed on Thursday afternoons and nights and offers no food on a Sunday evening. It is possible to camp in the village for a few euros (enquire at the Auberge de Couvige). A new *gîte d'étape* opened in the village in 2007. There are also two *chambres d'hôte* in Le Bouchet-Saint-Nicolas.

An attractive location to spend the night would be the Chalet Hôtel du Lac du Bouchet, which is visited on the excursion to Lac du Bouchet (open Easter to the end of September).

TRAVELS WITH A DONKEY

Modestine was reluctant to climb the 'interminable hill' out of Goudet (modern wayfarers may sympathise) and Stevenson became frustrated and exhausted with his efforts to coax the animal into a reasonable pace. To make matters worse, the enormous pack on the donkey's back would not remain upright and RLS was forced to carry several items of equipment himself. He thus had no hands free to control Modestine, and was ridiculed by passers-by in his pathetic attempts to prevent the donkey from entering every house and courtyard in the village of Ussel. He soon decided to jettison several items of his kit, including the leg of cold mutton and the egg whisk. But his troubles were by no means over as he headed west to Costaros, which he described as 'an ugly village on the highroad'.

From Costaros Stevenson tried in vain to reach Lac du Bouchet, where he had intended to camp for the night. His map and/or his ability to read it were insufficient and he received little advice from surly passers-by. Moreover, he was still having desperate problems with Modestine and her backpack, which fell to the ground for the second time on that first day. Thoroughly exhausted, less from walking than from thrashing Modestine, Stevenson arrived at Le Bouchet-Saint-Nicolas where he spent the night at an *auberge*.

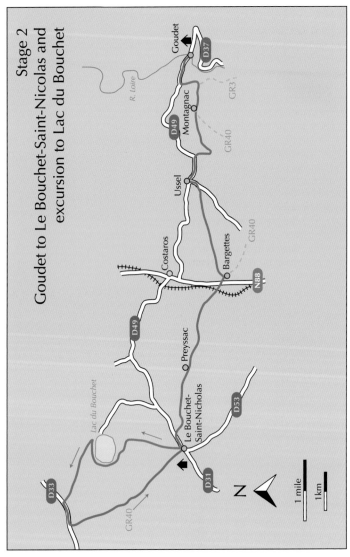

Stage 2
Goudet to Le Bouchet-Saint-Nicolas and
excursion to Lac du Bouchet

ROUTE

Leave **Goudet** by crossing the road bridge over the Loire and walk uphill on the D49, with the campsite below on the banks of the Loire. After about 600 metres you will reach a parking area on the left. ▶ The RLS Trail takes the track that descends from the parking area to cross a bridge and then climbs steeply. The track soon narrows and becomes stony, heading southwards. The very steep gradient eases for a while and the path becomes sandy.

Eventually a tree decorated with numerous way-marks is reached, including the old blue waymark for the RLS Trail. Ignore a red-and-white waymark for the GR3, which continues to the south, by descending on a path on the left. The GR70, along with the GR40, turns to the right, westwards, ascending the sandy track ahead. Remain on the main track (good views down to the Loire and the château) as it zigzags and eventually levels to arrive at a large barn at a bend in a road. Turn right on this lane to enter the village of **Montagnac**.

The car park is for visitors to the Château de Beaufort, which if open is worth a short visit before continuing on your way. To reach the gates of the château take the path that climbs sharply to the left.

Looking down to Goudet on the climb to Montagnac

Walk through Montagnac, noting the tiny chapel with bell on the left. Before the end of the village bear right at a red-and-white waymark for the GR70 (the GR40, which remains on the main road, parts company here). On leaving the village the poorly surfaced road becomes a sandy track that climbs and bends to the left. Nearing the top of the climb, bear left on the main track, ignoring another off to the right. The track levels; remain on it to reach the D54 road.

Stevenson visited the village of Ussel where '…saddle and all, the whole hypothec turned round and grovelled in the dust below the donkey's belly'.

Turn right on this road, descending on it to cross a road bridge over a river (the Ruisseau des Fouragettes) and then ascending to the junction with the D49, 800 metres before **Ussel**. Turn left on the D49, pass a stone cross on your right and continue into Ussel to arrive at a stone cross in the centre of the village. ◄ If requiring refreshment, then turn right to find a café/restaurant and also the village church, but the RLS Trail bears left on the D49 signposted to Landos.

Walk through Ussel village until, near the outskirts, by a **stone cross**, ① turn right on a red earthen track. After about 150 metres, at an open area, bear left onto a grassy track to pass an underground reservoir to reach another red earthen track. Turn left here for 50 metres to a track T-junction. Turn right and remain on this track for just over 2km to a little before the small village/hamlet of **Bargettes**. On this section distant Mont Mézenc can be seen to the east. ① The small town of **Costaros** comes into view over to the right. When the houses of Bargettes are seen ahead, leave the main track, which swings to the left, but continue ahead on an enclosed earthen track to Bargettes.

Turn right on the road in the tiny village, but then immediately left on a minor lane to walk through the hamlet. Twenty-five metres before reaching the N88, a busy main road, bear right to the road underpass. Once on the other side of the N88 bear right to climb with a large house on your left, to reach the old disused railway line (Le Puy to Langogne) at the old station building, now a private house. Those wanting the facilities of Costaros should turn right along the old railway track (signposted as the Circuit d'Ussel, yellow waymark). But for the GR70 cross the railway track and head uphill on an earthen track.

The track passes between two ancient volcanic hills, that of Le Pechay and La Gardine. Keep ahead, ignoring a track off to the right. About 1km after the D88, just after a stand of pine trees on your right, you will reach a track T-junction; here turn right, heading towards the wooded hill of Mont Marelle. After further 250 metres, immediately below the Marelle hill, turn left at another track T-junction, now heading towards **Preyssac**. ⓘ Veer right for about 50 metres when you enter

Carved stone doorway, Le Bouchet-Saint-Nicolas

the hamlet, and then leave the surfaced track by turning left onto an earthen track. After a further few hundred metres be sure to take the left branch at a track Y-junction, signposted to Le Bouchet-Saint-Nicolas.

The trail climbs a little (large quarry over to the right) to reach a high-level plateau, where the church and houses of **Le Bouchet-Saint-Nicolas** ⓘ come into view. Walk towards the village on a pleasant grassy track, soon bearing right at a track Y-junction. Later the track swings sharply to the left for 100 metres and then right again to maintain direction. The D31 road is met at a stone crucifix. Turn left along this road to enter Le Bouchet-Saint-Nicolas.

EXCURSION TO LAC DU BOUCHET

Although RLS failed to locate **Lac du Bouchet**, ⓘ today it is easy to find, and a visit is recommended. Leave Le Bouchet-Saint-Nicolas by taking the minor road heading north to the **Croix de la Chèvre** ⓘ ('Cross of the Goat'). From here take the road and later the track descending to

73

the lakeside. The walking trail around the lake is known as the Sentier de Garou. Refreshments may be obtained at the hotel/restaurant (Chalet Hôtel du Lac du Bouchet, open Easter to the end of September) on the far bank of the lake, reached by this pleasant lakeside path. For a circular walk back to Le Bouchet-Saint-Nicolas, the GR40 *variante* can be followed from behind the restaurant, following a path through the trees to the northwest, eventually crossing a minor road to reach the D33 at spot height 1243. Turn left here, and after about 400 metres, at the **Roman Road** (**Voie Romaine**) ① turn left again to follow it and the GR40 back into Le Bouchet-Saint-Nicolas.

Carved bear by Lac du Bouchet

POINTS OF INTEREST

Communal Ovens
The hamlets of Montagnac and Cros Pouget, the latter off-route south of Ussel, both contain fine examples of roadside ovens, used until recent times by the whole community for baking bread. They are nowadays only used at the time of the village fête. Other examples of communal life can also be seen in these now depopulated villages of the Velay, for example the bells on the roof of the village elder's house, used to summon the villagers together. One of the houses (rather hidden) in Cros Pouget has an interesting stone carving of the face of a woman. It is dated 1639 and thought by locals to represent that of the queen Marie de Medicis.

Wayside Crosses
A number of stone and metal wayside crosses will be seen along today's route and on the rest of the journey south. Some are many centuries old and have varying types of ornamentation. These ancient wayside markers, protecting travellers from the evils of the road, are particularly common in the Auvergne, Velay and Cévennes. They often mark important crossroads.

Views of Mont Mézenc
There are opportunities on today's walk for distant retrospective views of Mont Mézenc in the east. 'The view looking back was singularly wild and sad; the Mézenc and the peaks beyond St Julien stood out in trenchant gloom against a cold glitter in the east.' Mont Mézenc, at 1753m (5747ft) the highest peak in this region of the Massif Central, can be climbed as a detour while walking the Tour of the Velay (see *Walks in Volcano Country*, details of which can be found in Appendix 4).

Preyssac
Note the interesting old contraption used for holding oxen while they were being shod. Oxen were often used to pull hay carts and the like. Several of these *metiers à*

Old stone carving of hunter, dogs and prey, Le Bouchet-Saint-Nicolas

vache, now museum pieces, can still be seen in the villages and hamlets of the Auvergne. Note also in this hamlet the handpump for raising water from the well.

Le Bouchet-Saint-Nicolas

Look out for the interesting stone carvings, dated 1810, on the old building opposite the car park of the Auberge de Couvige, in the centre of the village. These depict a huntsman and animals. The latter could represent rabbits or hares, or perhaps even the terrifying 18th-century 'Bête du Gévaudan' (see Stage 5, Points of Interest, Gévaudan). There are more carvings on the back and side of the building, as well as elsewhere in the village.

Roman Road

A Roman road, La Voie Bollène, several kilometres in length, runs northwest–southeast through Le Bouchet-Saint-Nicolas, and is used to return to the village from Lac du Bouchet. It can be followed as a track (the GR40) through the Lac du Bouchet forest, all the way to Montbonnet in the north, a distance of some 12km.

Croix de la Chèvre

The Croix de la Chèvre ('Cross of the Goat'), on the way
to Lac du Bouchet, is decorated with a carved goat's
head. Legend has it that a village once existed near the
site of this cross. One night the inhabitants, with the
exception of an old woman and her goat, refused to give
hospitality to a beggar. In revenge the beggar cursed the
village and as a result it was engulfed by water, and all,
save the woman and goat, were lost. It is said that at
times the ruins of the village can be seen beneath the
lake and that at night the church bell can be heard dole-
fully ringing.

Lac du Bouchet

One of several volcanic lakes in the Velay, it is 28m (92ft)
deep, covers an area of approximately 43 hectares and
has a diameter of about 800 metres. It occupies the site
of a crater created by an immense volcanic explosion.
Other notable volcanic lakes in the area include that of
Saint Front, north of Mont Mézenc, and the Lac
d'Issarlès, southeast of the village of the same name.

*Restored plough at Le
Bouchet-Saint-Nicolas*

STAGE 3 – Le Bouchet-Saint-Nicolas to Pradelles

21km (13 miles)
5hrs 10mins

Location	Distance (km)		Time (hr min)	
	Section	Cum	Section	Cum
Le Bouchet-Saint-Nicolas (1218m)	0.0	0.0	0 00	0 00
Landos	6.3	6.3	1 35	1 35
Jagonas	3.2	9.5	0 45	2 20
Arquejol	2.3	11.8	0 35	2 55
Rocher de la Fagette (1265m)	7.0	18.8	1 40	4 35
Pradelles (1110m)	2.2	21.0	0 35	5 10

An ancient track over a high-level plateau leads to the rather uninteresting small market town of Landos. An excellent walk follows, to the hamlets of Jagonas and then Arquejol, where will be seen the first of two monumental railway viaducts encountered on the RLS Trail. A short detour from the RLS Trail leads to the summit of the Rocher de la Fagette, from where there is a good view down to historic Pradelles, said by some to be the prettiest village in all France.

FACILITIES

At Landos food can be bought from street stalls on market day, and otherwise there is a choice of shops and a supermarket. The town has a small selection of café/bars, a hotel/restaurant and a bank.

Pradelles has a good selection of shops, supermarkets, bars, cafés and restaurants. There are two hotels, a post office and a bank in town. The new *gîte d'étape* in Pradelles, opened in 2005, is in a charming traditional building in the old part of the town. It has three rooms – a two-bed, a four-bed and a six-bed, as well as a few

Market day in Landos

extra mattresses for use when times are busy. The tourist office is in the Place de Foirail near the Place de la Halle in the centre. This office will supply a free street map and has details of the history of Pradelles, the annual *son et lumière* and Stevenson's connection with the town. An overnight stay in Pradelles is a must!

TRAVELS WITH A DONKEY

RLS was well received at the inn at Le Bouchet-Saint-Nicolas, where he found himself, much to his embarrassment, sharing a room with a married couple. The next morning the landlord presented him with a goad, a stick with a sharp pin at the end, which Stevenson found most effective in encouraging Modestine to follow the path. Thus equipped he continued to Pradelles, finding the road 'dead solitary all the way'. RLS gave no indication of his route to Pradelles, but it was probably along what is now the D53 and N88.

'Pradelles stands on a hillside, high above the Allier, surrounded by rich meadow...It was a cheerless prospect, but one stimulating to a traveller'. RLS was now skirting the western rim of old Vivarais, leaving the Velay to enter Gévaudan, home a century earlier to the fabulous 'Bête du Gévaudan', a huge wolf – or even werewolf – which reputedly 'ate women and children and shepherdesses celebrated for their beauty'. Wolves

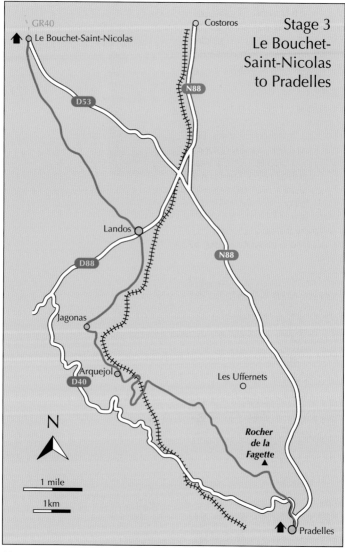

GR40
Le Bouchet-Saint-Nicolas

Costoros

Stage 3
Le Bouchet-
Saint-Nicolas
to Pradelles

D53

N88

Landos

D88

N88

Jagonas

Arquejol

Les Uffernets

D40

N

Rocher
de la
Fagette

1 mile

1km

Pradelles

still roamed this remote, desolate country in the late 19th century and this was no doubt the main reason for including the revolver in his saddle pack. (The modern traveller need have no such worries and is advised to leave any firearms at home!)

ROUTE

In the centre of **Le Bouchet-Saint-Nicolas**, bear left at the Stevenson and Modestine statue, signposted as the Chemin de Stevenson to Landos. Exit the village on this wide surfaced lane, passing a stone cross on your right. After about a kilometre, near a small reservoir on your right, bear left at a track Y-junction. Follow this dirt/cinder track southeastwards, ignoring any tracks coming in from the left or right. The trail crosses a flat high-level plateau. After several kilometres the track bends to the right (ignore the track on the left here) to join a minor surfaced lane in about 40 metres, by a solitary tree on your left.

Ancient cross outside Landos

Turn left on this narrow road, which eventually descends, passes picnic tables and reaches the outskirts of the town of **Landos**. ① On reaching a T-junction by a picturesque packhorse bridge (Pont de la Castier, restored in 1989) turn right on the road, passing the Lavoir de la Fontanille (restored in 1997) and La Fontanille itself (restored in 2000, non-drinking water) to enter Landos.

At the crossroads and square in Landos, turn right for a few metres. Immediately after the *hôtel de ville*, turn left along a small street. Walk ahead at a crossroads on the outskirts of the town. In about 400 metres take a fork off to the right on a grassy track. Follow this for another 400 metres to a track T-junction at a stone cross, near to a **railway line**. ① Here turn right on a track with a fence on the right. This leads to a T-junction of tracks where you turn left and in 30 metres turn sharp right on the upper of two tracks.

In a further 130 metres, when the track forks, take the left-hand (minor) fork (railway line below to the left). Walk along this track on an embankment with a hedgerow on the right. At a T-junction turn right and continue along this track to the hamlet of **Jagonas**. ◄

The distant hills are the Cévennes, where the RLS Trail is heading.

Pass a barn complex on your right, then immediately before the first building on the left turn left. Stay on the surfaced track and remain on this as it swings to the left. On reaching a triple track junction, take the left fork (Stevenson waymark) descending to cross a stream. Climb on this poorly surfaced track until its swings to the left. Here leave this track by turning right on an earthen track. After a few minutes, at a track junction, be sure to take a left fork on a grassy enclosed track.

Just before reaching the hamlet of **Arquejol** the track becomes surfaced. Descend towards the hamlet. At a road T-junction turn left and in a few metres swing right towards the buildings. Keep to the right of a triangular area of grass (with picnic table) in the centre of Arquejol.

At the far end of Arquejol, turn left as indicated by red-and-white and green-and-white waymarks, descending on a grit track into the deep valley below. Soon the spectacular 11-arched redundant Arquejol viaduct, which carried the railway high above the river, comes into view. ▶ Descend to cross a stream by a small stone bridge and then climb on the cinder track with good views back to Arquejol, situated on top of the hill.

On reaching an open area ignore the enclosed track bearing slightly to the right, but instead bear a little towards the left to pick up a cinder track which climbs very gently, aiming for the railway seen ahead on the left. Pass under a railway bridge and immediately turn left (Stevenson 'Lions Club of Le Puy' signpost) to follow a wide grassy track alongside a railway line.

Soon the latter swings to the left to pass over the viaduct, but our trail turns to the right to begin a long and steep climb on a good track. When the trail levels out ignore a track that descends to the right, but continue ahead (another 'Stevenson' sign), soon climbing again, but this time more gently. The track eventually levels and then descends gently to the D284; cross over to take the gravel track signposted to Le Cros.

Although the river is fairly small, there is quite a deep gorge at this point and it was a considerable feat of engineering to span the valley.

Walker on the route out of Arquejol

This is an excellent balcony route, offering, over to the right, fine views of distant ridges and the large Naussac reservoir near Langogne.

After about 100 metres bear left onto a sandy track heading towards trees. ◄ In about a further kilometre pass under high-tension electricity cables to reach a cross-tracks. Continue ahead on a grassy track, and remain on it as it descends and swings to the right to meet another track. Turn right on this for a few metres and then left uphill ('Stevenson' sign) to reach a sandy red earthen track at a bend in the latter.

Turn right to continue the ascent. The track heads southeastwards for about a kilometre before entering woodland and then veering northeast for about 400 metres. Ignore a track off to the right and then emerge into an open area just below the rocks of the summit of the **Rocher de la Fagette**. ⓘ By means of a short detour from the official route of the GR70, it is easily possible to climb from here to the summit of this fine viewpoint.

To do so, pass through an electrified fence at the access point, and a fairly easy scramble of less than 10 minutes duration brings you to the summit, where there is an IGN triangulation point and a tremendous view of the surrounding countryside, including the village of Les Uffernets to the nort-northwest and Pradelles, your destination for the night, to the south-southeast. ◄

Note Take care on the route to the summit, as there may be excessive vegetation covering the rocks, which can hide ankle-wrenching holes, and possibly vipers – beware of the possibility of surprising the latter.

Return to the RLS Trail, and where the wood on your right comes to an end, turn right at a track junction to follow a grassy track, which soon becomes a narrow footpath heading south-southeast back into the trees. Keep ahead at a track junction in the woods, heading down to the southeast towards **Pradelles**. Emerge from the woods to reach the D40 at a bend. Turn left along this road to enter Pradelles.

Turn right on the N88 at the crossroads in Pradelles and walk into the centre of the town. Bear right at the war memorial into the Place de la Halle. Pass firstly the large and historic Fontaine du Melon (the oldest fountain in Pradelles), and then the birthplace of Jeanne La Verde, before bearing left at the Portail de la Verdette into Rue du Mazel. You are now in the very heart of the historic old town.

POINTS OF INTEREST

Ancient track heading towards Pradelles

Landos
The village is built on the edge of an ancient volcanic crater.

The Railway
The Le Puy to Langogne disused railway line is encountered on several occasions on this section of the walk, principally at Bargettes, Landos and Arquejol. The line, built by the engineer Paul Séjourné, was opened in October 1912, long after Stevenson came this way, and provided a direct route between Langogne and Paris. It was closed to passenger traffic in 1939, but still used for freight until 1 April 1988. The line crossed a number of bridges, the viaduct (seen from the RLS Trail) at Arquejol in particular representing a remarkable engineering achievement. The redundant line joins the operational Paris to Nîmes main line just north of Langogne.

Following the old railway

After the closure of the line, the rails from Le Puy through Brives-Charensac to Solignac-sur-Loire were lifted to convert the route to a pleasant grassy walking and cycling track. It is possible to walk or cycle along the track all the way from Le Puy to Landos. Many of the station buildings (e.g. the station at Landos) are still in existence.

The rails between Landos and Langogne are still in place, however, and used these days for a tourist *vélo-rail* (the sort of open trucks on rails often seen in old cowboy movies, which are pumped up and down to provide movement) – a recommended day out!

Rocher de la Fagette

A summit at 1265m (4147ft) to the northwest of Pradelles. The GR70 passes close to this peak, which is a superb viewpoint.

STAGE 4 – *Pradelles to Langogne*

6.4km (4 miles)
1hr 35mins

Location	Distance (km)		Time (hr min)	
	Section	**Cum**	**Section**	**Cum**
Pradelles (1110m)	0.0	0.0	0 00	0 00
River Allier	5.2	5.2	1 15	1 15
Langogne (915m)	1.2	6.4	0 20	1 35

A very short walk today, the shortest on the whole trail, and little more than an easy stroll. The reason for this is to allow plenty of time to explore picturesque and historic Pradelles before leaving for Langogne. Thankfully the main road into the centre of Langogne is avoided by a walk through the quieter suburbs of the town, near the railway line.

FACILITIES

There are three hotels in Langogne, another by Lac de Naussac, and at least one *chambre d'hôte* in the town. Langogne has two campsites, the nearest and least pretentious (one star) is about 800 metres to the east of the town centre, between the railway line and the river. The other is the Camping de Naussac, near to the reservoir on the other side of the town (follow the road signs).

The largest settlement on the whole of the RLS Trail, Langogne has an abundance of cafés, bars, restaurants, shops of most types and supermarkets, as well as banks, a post office and tourist office. The town is on the main line railway between Paris and Nîmes. There are several trains a day to Clermont-Ferrand and Paris (Gare de Lyon), and also to La Bastide, Alès and Nîmes (for connections to Marseille, Nice, Montpellier, Toulouse, Bordeaux and Avignon). The best bus services on the whole trail operate from here, with services to Mende and to Pradelles, Landos, Costaros and Le Puy. Buses stop in the high street in the centre of town and at the railway station (SNCF), outside the Café du Midi.

TRAVELS WITH A DONKEY

RLS stayed for less than an hour in Pradelles, omitted to see the Notre Dame de Pradelles, 'who performed many miracles, although she was of wood', and was soon 'goading Modestine down the steep descent that leads to Langogne on the Allier…The long-promised rain was beginning to fall' as he crossed the bridge and entered the town. Despite all the problems with Modestine and her heavy burden, and his incompetent map reading, Stevenson had walked all the way from Le Monastier to Langogne in just two days. This supreme effort was to tell in the days that followed as the pair became more fatigued and travel weary.

ROUTE

Note the Saint Andrew's Cross (dating from the 1978 centenary year waymarking of the route) in the Place de la Halle in **Pradelles**. ⓘ It looks somewhat dilapidated now, but is still clearly seen, and is one of the few remaining such signs along the trail. There is also a sign here indicating the Stevenson Trail to Langogne.

Take the Rue du Mazel downhill under an archway, the Portail du Besset, to join the Rue Basse exiting the old village. Continue to the cemetery at the Place Père Charles Boyer. Ignore the left turn at the end of the cemetery (the Chemin de Régordane), but continue ahead on a wide grassy track. Cross the D28 and go ahead down an earthen track. Remain on this for 1.5km. At a junction of three tracks, take the middle one, which has a surface of volcanic ash and is bordered by hedgerows. Pass a house on your right, where there are several wonderfully restored and painted old ploughs in the garden, and continue on the track until it meets a road at a bend in the latter.

Turn left downhill on this minor road to reach the main N88. Turn right to pass a picnic area (l'aire de

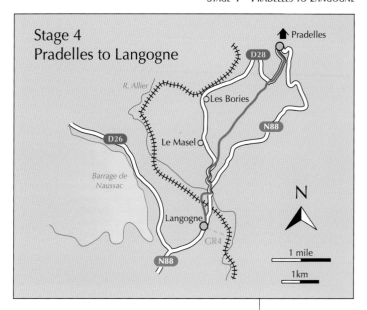

Stage 4
Pradelles to Langogne

pique-nique) and information boards describing points of interest in Langogne and in the *département* of Lozère, which you are now entering. Turn right to cross the bridge over the **Allier**, so entering the outskirts of **Langogne**. ⓘ

Immediately turn right on the Quartier des Abattoirs. After about 200 metres turn left to pass under the railway line by means of a long tunnel. Turn left at the far end of the tunnel to stay on the surfaced lane. This quiet road, the Rue des Cités, swings to the right and passes a metal crucifix dated 1898.

At a cemetery continue ahead (i.e. ignore Rue Henri Guigon on the right) along a one-way street into the Avenue de la Gare and on into the Rue des Capucins. This leads to the *hôtel de ville* and *office de tourisme*. Bear left to reach the main road, Boulevard General de Gaulle. Turn right along this main street to continue the RLS Trail. After about 150 metres the RLS Trail takes a

Market Hall, Langogne

small lane on the left, the Rue du Pont Vieux, but to visit the *halle* (the old covered market) continue along the main road for a further 50 metres.

POINTS OF INTEREST

Pradelles

There should be plenty time in the morning for exploring the charming medieval hill town of Pradelles, which has been declared a classified site of historical importance. Pradelles has the feel of a town, although it is technically a very large village, with narrow streets, idyllic squares and many fine old traditional buildings. Places of interest include the 17th-century church, the château and the remains of the town ramparts. There are also several pleasant water fountains in the town.

The history of the town goes back a long way. In the 12th century a band of thieves and bandits, under the leadership of one Captain Chambaud, frequently

attacked the towns and villages in the area. The day they
tried to enter the walled town of Pradelles, they ran into
resistance from a woman called La Verdette (named after
the part of the town in which she lived). She was so
incensed at the assailants that she picked up a stone from
the Porte de la Verdette (one of the town gateways) and
threw it at the captain, incapacitating him. His men ran
off and the woman was declared a heroine. La Verdette's
famous deed is commemorated in a painting in the

*Statue of St Gilles,
Pradelles*

91

Chapelle Notre-Dame, Pradelles

Notre-Dame church and in a stone mural (erected in 1988) in the Rue du Mazel. Every year for two weeks in July/August the Fêtes Historiques de Pradelles is held, a spectacular pageant in which the history of the town is re-enacted.

The church, or Chapelle Notre-Dame, at the southern end of the town was built by the Dominicans in 1613, restored from 1867 to 1876, then again in a more recent restoration beginning in 2006. The famous 'miraculous Virgin of Pradelles' (Notre Dame de Pradelles) was brought back to France by a crusader and found on this site in 1512, hence the Chapelle Notre-Dame was built here in honour of her. The Virgin was said to perform a variety of miracles, and so attracted a large number of pilgrims. The wooden statue, clothed in a white dress, can be seen at the far end of the church.

The main and largest church in the village is simply called the parish church and was renovated in 1999, when new and modern Stations of the Cross paintings were commissioned. The church also contains a 1949 replica of the Notre Dame de Pradelles. The Musée Vivant du Cheval de Trail, celebrating the working horses from this region, is located behind the parish church (open from April to the end of September).

If the day is a sunny one, be sure to locate the small hill to the southwest of the village, near the cemetery and the Croix d'Ardenne. There is an excellent view of ancient Pradelles from here, and in the late afternoon the sun will be in the best position for photographs. Also locate the *table d'orientation*, built on the small rise on the southeast side of the town in the millennium year 2000. This indicates the direction of several of the places to the south that you will visit later on the RLS Trail, including the highest point on the route, the Pic de Finiels (Stage 8), and the Trappist monastery of Notre-Dames-des-Neiges (Stage 6).

For those wishing to stay awhile in Pradelles, but still wanting to walk, there is a circular walking tour of the surrounding countryside – the Circuit Pédestre du Mazonric (PR125). It is 19km (11.8 miles) long and timed at 4hrs 45mins. The walk starts from the junction of the D40 and N88 and is waymarked throughout with yellow paint stripes.

Langogne
The town is mostly modern and semi-industrial, but dates originally from the 11th century. The old bridge across the Allier and the covered market (*halle*), built in 1742, are of interest, as is the very fine 12th-century church.

Reservoir de Naussac
Langogne is attracting more tourists these days, since the flooding of the wide, fertile Naussac plain after the completion of a dam in the early 1980s. The landscape here, which remained largely unchanged for a century after Stevenson's visit, has now been completely transformed with the formation of this artificial lake. The reservoir

Langogne

covers an area of about 1100 hectares and provides a shoreline of some 40km (25 miles) in length. There is now a waymarked trail around the reservoir, the Tour du Lac (blue-and-white waymarks). This is torturous and slow in parts as it negotiates the ups and downs through the woods around the lakeside, and in wet weather some areas become very marshy. There are beaches for sunbathing, while the more active can swim, windsurf, fish or hire pedalos.

STAGE 5 – *Langogne to Cheylard-l'Évêque*

15.8km (9.8 miles)
4hrs 10mins

Location	Distance (km)		Time (hr. min)	
	Section	Cum	Section	Cum
Langogne (915m)	0.0	0.0	0 00	0 00
Saint-Flour-de-Mercoire	6.8	6.8	1 45	1 45
Sagne-Rousse	3.3	10.1	0 50	2 35
Fouzillac	2.0	12.1	0 40	3 15
Fouzillic	0.5	12.6	0 05	3 20
Cheylard-l'Évêque (1126m)	3.2	15.8	0 50	4 10

There should be some time for a further look around Langogne before leaving the town to head southwest for Cheylard-l'Évêque. But be sure not to leave too late in the day, as Stevenson did, in case you too are forced into an unforeseen 'camp in the dark'. After the village of Saint-Flour-de-Mercoire the route traverses quite remote countryside, where it is not hard to imagine that in the absence of modern waymarking and without a guidebook and map the way could very easily be lost.

FACILITIES

None of the villages and hamlets between Langogne and Cheylard-l'Évêque has anything in the way of facilities for the traveller. Twenty years ago the same was true in the small village of Cheylard-l'Évêque, but now happily the wayfarer is well provided for with a combined *chambre d'hôte* and *gîte d'étape*, the Refuge du Moure, located opposite the small church in the centre of the village. Excellent meals are on offer here. A café is also nearby, but there is no shop in Cheylard.

TRAVELS WITH A DONKEY

Stevenson spent the morning of his third day writing up his journal and it was not until 2.30pm that he set off from Langogne. The weather was poor: 'All the way up the long hill from Langogne it rained and hailed alternatively; the wind kept freshening steadily…plentiful hurrying clouds…careered out of the north and followed me along my way.' He reached the hamlet of Sagne-Rousse by 4pm, but for the next few hours wandered lost in the fir woods to the southwest. Both the adults and children he encountered gave him no assistance: '[They] did not care a stalk of parsley if I wandered all night upon the hills!'

At long last, the dusk now rapidly gathering, he arrived at Fouzillic, 'three houses on a hillside, near a wood of birches'. Here he was put on the right course for Cheylard, but soon darkness fell: 'I have been abroad in many a black night, but never in a blacker…the sky was simply darkness overhead…roaring blackness.' Stumbling about in the darkness he reached a second hamlet, that of Fouzillac, actually further from his destination than Fouzillic. He called at a house offering money to pay for a guide to Cheylard, but assistance was refused and he therefore had no alternative but to 'camp in the dark'. He was wet from the rain of the afternoon and had neither water nor bread for himself. His evening meal consisted of one of the tins of Bologna sausages and a cake of chocolate, all washed down with neat brandy!

Despite his privations, RLS appeared to have enjoyed the experience. When he awoke, 'The world was flooded with a blue light, mother of the dawn…I was surprised to find how easy and pleasant it had been, even in this tempestuous weather…I had felt not a touch of cold, and awakened with unusually lightsome and clear sensations.' With assistance from an old man in Fouzillic, he was soon 'within sight of Cheylard, the destination I had hunted for so long'.

ROUTE

About 150 metres after turning right (south) on the
Boulevard General de Gaulle in **Langogne**, leave it for a
small lane on the left, the Rue du Pont Vieux, opposite
the Portail Sud, the south gate of the old town. Cross the
old bridge to reach a GR4/GR70 junction. Turn right
along the GR70. Bear left at a main road, now heading
out of town on the D906. After about 150 metres turn
right into Rue du 11 Novembre 1918, signposted to the
'Stade'. Pass this stadium and the road sign indicating the
town limit of Langogne, 60 metres after which, at a Y-
junction, bear left signposted to Brugerolles, and to
Cheylard-l'Évêque in 15km.

After about a kilometre, where this minor road
swings sharply to the left to enter Brugerolles, leave it by
bearing right onto a sandy track. Gradually climb on this
track. Shortly after it levels, about 800 metres from leaving the road, bear right at a track junction (GR70 waymark). ▸ After about half a kilometre, on entering a

*Restored house in
Fouzillac*

Note that the GR700,
the Chemin de
Régordane, continues
ahead at this point.

97

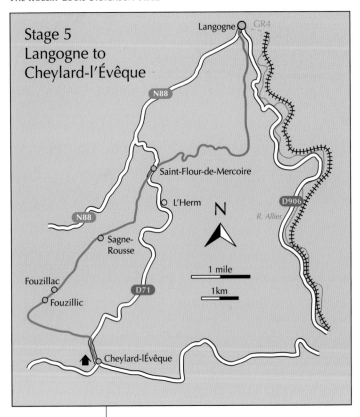

Stage 5
Langogne to
Cheylard-l'Évêque

Langogne   GR4

N88

Saint-Flour-de-Mercoire

L'Herm

N

N88

Sagne-
Rousse

R. Allier

D906

Fouzillac

Fouzillic

D71

1 mile

1km

Cheylard-l'Évêque

pine wood, turn right at a track T-junction (look back at this point for a distant view of Pradelles).

Reach and cross over a minor road, following a signpost for Le Monteil. On reaching the first building of this hamlet turn left at a red-and-white arrow onto a sandy track, with a fence on the right, soon entering trees. This ancient trail through the woods meanders on its descent to a stream, and then continues to the valley bottom to cross the River Langouyrou by a stone bridge. A steep climb follows on a surfaced lane to reach the

small village of **Saint-Flour-de-Mercoire**, ⓘ passing two metal roadside crosses on the way.

Saint-Flour-de-Mercoire

On reaching the second cross, at a water fountain, turn right for 100 metres to visit the ancient village **church**, which is well worth the short detour. Note the ancient gravestones laid flat as a path up to the church door. (The ugly modern housing estate was not here on my first visit in 1988.)

Turn left at the T-junction in the centre of the village, by the *mairie* and at a black statue of Saint-Flour. Continue on this road (ignoring a blue waymark on the right, opposite a metal cross, after 75 metres – this is old route of the RLS Trail) to pass the road sign indicating the limit of the village. Where the road swings sharply to the left, turn right onto a dirt track (GR70 signpost indicating Sagne-Rousse in 2km). This trail climbs and enters the Bois de la Garde. On reaching a track T-junction at the top of the climb, by a concrete electricity pylon, turn left into the wood.

After a few hundred metres ignore a track off to the left but continue with trees on your right. This track soon swings to the right (GR70 waymark on a tree). When you reach a clearing, take the middle of three tracks, soon with a low stone wall on the left and a fence on the right. Remain on this track when the latter disappear. Barbed-wire fences appear on both sides before the track comes to a road. Turn left here to walk into the hamlet of **Sagne-Rousse**. ①

Walk straight ahead at the metal cross, signposted to Laubarnès and Cheylard-L'Évêque, but after the solitary house on the right take the track off to the right. After several hundred metres, pass an interesting small stone cross on a boulder in a field on the right. Reach and pass through a large metal gate and continue ahead, through the wood to pass through a second metal gate. The trail becomes a thin footpath through the trees. Continue on this on a magnetic bearing of 220 degrees.

These two rather nondescript hamlets owe entirely to RLS's navigational incompetence any fame they may now enjoy!

Cross the Cham stream, which is followed by a marshy area. Be careful not to lose the line of the red-and-white waymarks hereabouts (remember RLS's problems!). After the wet area, follow a clearer path to the right of a barbed-wire fence. Walk ahead at a barbed-wire 'gate' and climb the small hill beyond on the track. Continue ahead to reach the road at **Fouzillac** (Fouzilhac), along which you turn left to reach **Fouzillic** (Fouzilhic) within 350 metres. ◄

Maintain direction, now on a track, but in about 300 metres turn left (south) at a cross-tracks onto a path. After a further 200 metres, at a Y-junction take the left-hand track, which soon becomes enclosed between hedgerows. The trail then becomes an ancient track deep within the woods. Soon after leaving the cover of the trees, turn right at a track T-junction. Later ignore a track to the right and continue ahead, eventually dropping to **Cheylard-l'Évêque**. ① Reach a main road, the D71, and follow it for a further 200 metres into the village. In the centre of Cheylard-l'Évêque you will reach a metal cross, the Croix de la Mission, dated 1827.

POINTS OF INTEREST

Gévaudan

Today the trail enters wildest Gévaudan, where even today there is a feeling of remoteness that is not experienced in the Velay. Despite the presence of a waymarked route, attention to detail with map and route description is required if the modern wayfarer is not to experience a fate similar to that of Stevenson, who became hopelessly lost in the neighbourhood of Fouzillac (or Fouzilhac) and Fouzillic (or Fouzilhic).

In Stevenson's day the land was exploited by sheep farmers, and as a result of animal over-population the landscape had become denuded and suffered from erosion. Human depopulation began with the First World War and has continued ever since, with the lure of more fruitful work in towns and cities. In this respect, the land is even more remote than it was over a century ago. Tourism, particularly rambling, horse and pony trekking

Looking down to Cheylard-l'Évêque

and cross-country skiing, are going some way towards revitalising the area.

During the 1760s the Beast (*Bête*) of Gévaudan roamed this desolate country. Most of the hundred or more killings attributed to the animal, the 'Napoléon Bonaparte of Wolves!', took place in the region between Langogne and Luc, the scene of today's walk. The story has it that the King of France himself eventually ordered a huntsman from Paris to track and kill the notorious wolf, which the huntsman did with the aid of a silver bullet.

Saint-Flour-de-Mercoire

The Romanesque church of Saint-Flour-de-Mercoire lies a short distance off-route, together with a rather sad memorial to the men of the district who died during the First World War. It is a world apart from this quiet backwater to the killing fields of northern France.

Ancient church of Saint-Flour-de-Mercoire

Sagne-Rousse

Between here and Cheylard-l'Évêque, RLS got lost. Scientists have discovered that this is an area where the magnetic field is disturbed because of faults and underground streams, and some have put forward this theory to explain RLS's navigational problems. However, during my two visits to the area, with a gap of 18 years in between, I found no compass deviations, and doubt this theory. The terrain is fairly easy to navigate today with good maps and waymarking, but without these aids it would have been easy to become disorientated, particularly as night was approaching for Stevenson.

Cheylard-l'Évêque

There is a small chapel, the 'diminutive and tottering church', in the village centre, but the principle religious monument to visit is Notre-Dame de Tous Graces (Our Lady of All the Graces), situated on a hill above the village and reached by a steep path that starts from the back of the Refuge du Moure and ascends past the twelve Stations of the Cross. A magnificent view rewards the effort of the climb, particularly down to Cheylard and northwards towards the village of Laubarnès, high up the wooded valley.

The old Mercoire abbey is located 3.2km south of Le Cheylard, just off the D71. A waymarked PR trail, the Circuit Pédestre de l'Évêque (6km, 2 hours), departs from the centre of the village for those who want to explore the neighbourhood further.

STAGE 6 – *Cheylard-l'Évêque via Notre-Dame-des-Neiges to La Bastide-Puylaurent*

23.4km (14.5 miles)
7hrs

Location	Distance (km)		Time (hr min)	
	Section	**Cum**	**Section**	**Cum**
Cheylard-l'Évêque (1126m)	0.0	0.0	0 00	0 00
Les Pradels (outskirts)	6.2	6.2	1 35	1 35
Lac de Louradou	2.2	8.4	0 35	2 10
Luc	4.2	12.6	1 05	3 15
Pranlac	1.5	14.1	0 25	3 40
Laveyrune	0.3	14.4	0 05	3 45
Rogleton	2.4	16.8	0 45	4 30
Notre-Dame-des-Neiges	3.6	20.4	1 30	6 00
La Bastide-Puylaurent (1016m)	3.0	23.4	1 00	7 00

On the walk across the Gévaudan between Cheylard-l'Évêque and Luc it is very easy to imagine the remoteness of this area of gentle, rounded wooded hills in centuries past. The famous white Madonna on the roof of the Château de Luc was brand new at the time of RLS's visit, but has stood on this spot ever since. Easy valley walking follows, before making a considerable detour and climb eastwards to visit the Trappist Monastère de Notre-Dame-des-Neiges, a highlight of the stage. The GR70 bypasses the monastery, but as it was such an integral part of Stevenson's journey and his subsequent book, a place he feared so much (or wanted his readership to think he feared), it is inconceivable to omit a visit here.

The walk over the hills and through the woods to the monastery is a good one, offering distant views of the surrounding countryside, and the monks are courteous, polite and informative, making for a pleasant visit. An hour's easy walking leads from the monastery to the small town of La Bastide-Puylaurent, where every facility needed by the traveller is on offer.

FACILITIES

Alas, the small 'open all hours' shop in Luc has now closed, but there is still a café in Luc where it may be possible to buy a meal. It is situated down by the river opposite the entrance to the campsite (the Camping Municipal 'Les Galets'), which is about 500 metres off-route. There are no places of refreshment between Cheylard and Luc and none in the small communities of Pranlac, Laveyrune and Rogleton. The monks at Notre-Dame-des-Neiges sell their produce in the abbey shop, where café refreshments may also be enjoyed. Although rooms are available at the abbey for travellers, prior booking is absolutely essential (The Hôtellerie du Monastère, tel 04.66.46.59.12).

La Bastide-Puylaurent has cafés and restaurants, in addition to three hotels and a *gîte d'étape*. The latter, which normally closes for the year in mid-September, is located opposite the railway station (trains on both the Nîmes to Paris Cévenol mainline and on the branch line to Mende via Chasseradès). Also in the town will be found a tourist office, supermarket, several other shops and a post office. The backpacker could stay at the camp-site, which is over 2km from La Bastide, signposted from both the town centre and from the GR70 (see Stage 7).

TRAVELS WITH A DONKEY

Stevenson was well received at the inn in Cheylard-l'Évêque, where he ate, drank and wrote his journal, before setting out for Luc on a road 'through one of the most beggarly countries in the world. It was like the worst of the Scotch Highlands, only worse…'. It was this section between Cheylard and Luc that prompted him to pen the most famous lines in the book, from which the quotation reproduced at the front of this guidebook is taken. 'Why anyone should desire to visit either Luc or Cheylard is more than my much-inventing spirit can suppose. For my part, I travel not to go anywhere, but to go. I travel for travel's sake. The great affair is to move; to feel the needs and hitches of our life more nearly; to come down off the feather-bed of civilisation, and find the

'Fifty quintals of white Madonna' at Château de Luc

globe granite underfoot and strewn with cutting flints.' (This quotation is often confused with the similar, 'To travel hopefully is a better thing than to arrive', but the latter appeared in an essay of 1881 entitled 'El Dorado'.)

RLS spent the night at Luc, 'a straggling double file of houses wedged between hill and river. It had no beauty, nor was there any notable feature, save the old castle overhead with its fifty quintals of brand-new Madonna.'

Stevenson had made considerable progress from Le Monastier, arriving at Luc after only four days of walking, and this with only a half-day from Langogne and enforced encampment near Fouzillac. He was to take several more half-days from now on, as he lingered to write up his journal and take prolonged rests. Both RLS and the donkey were by now suffering from the physical demands of the journey, and his inexperience at walking was evident, as he had made the mistake of going too far and too fast, too early in the expedition. Modestine in particular was in a very sorry state '...there were her two forelegs no better than raw beef on the inside, and blood was running from under her tail'. The modern traveller following the suggested stages in this guidebook is at present some two days behind Stevenson's itinerary, but we, like him, are to finish after 12 days on the road, hopefully in a far better state than RLS and his four-legged companion.

Stevenson set out from Luc on his fifth day after leaving Le Monastier, having first rearranged Modestine's saddle pack yet again. He followed the valley of the Allier, noting that the railway that ran beside the river (the Paris–Nîmes line) was 'the only bit of railway in Gévaudan, although there are many proposals afoot and surveys being made, and...a station standing already built in Mende'. He was, of course, referring to the branch line from La Bastide to Mende, which is still operational today and which is followed on the RLS Trail from Chasseradès to L'Estampe. The pair continued along the valley, first to La Bastide, where RLS was then directed to 'follow a road that mounted on the left [the journal erroneously states 'upon my right'] among the hills of Vivarais, the modern Ardèche'.

For a man of Stevenson's Protestant background the Monastery of Notre-Dame-des-Neiges held unknown horrors. 'I have rarely approached anything with more unaffected terror than the monastery of our Lady of the Snows...fear took hold on me from head to foot.' He first encountered one Father Apollinaris, who escorted him to the gates of the monastery, where, as a literary man, Stevenson was graciously received by Father Michael, the father-hospitaller. He was wined and dined and spoke with several of the Trappist monks, who, while waiting on a stranger, were allowed to speak. He was given a guided tour of the monastery by an Irish deacon named Michael O'Callaghan, and attended compline and salve regina at the end of the day, before returning to his spartan room, 'clean and whitewashed, and furnished with strict necessities'. His slumber was disturbed by the first bell of the day at 2am.

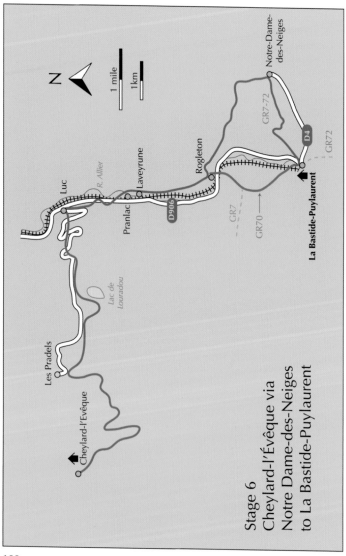

Stage 6
Cheylard-l'Évêque via
Notre Dame-des-Neiges
to La Bastide-Puylaurent

ROUTE

Walk through the village of **Cheylard-l'Évêque**, noting the 'diminutive and tottering' church on the left to which RLS referred (see Cheylard-l'Évêque, Places if Interest, Stage 5). Cross the bridge over the Cheylard river and begin the climb out of the village on the D71. About 50 metres after a *maison forestière* on the left, bear left on a dirt track that climbs to enter the forest. Later ignore a grassy track on the right, but stay on the main dirt track that climbs to a Y-junction where you take the left-hand branch, still heading uphill.

On reaching a track T-junction in the middle of the forest turn left (GR70 and a PR waymark). The track swings to the northeast. At an oblique cross-tracks turn right, now heading downhill and soon swinging to the right (south). Ignore a track off to the right that climbs steeply, but continue downhill to the southeast. Later swing to the left at another track junction. Always keep to the main track, which is well waymarked. Descend all the way to a road.

Turn right on this road to descend to cross a stream (the Ruisseau de Langouyrou again) by a concrete bridge. Now begin a long climb towards the hamlet of **Les Pradels**. After 150 metres leave the road by taking a grassy track on the right. This cuts off a road zigzag. Cross the road again and ahead on the track opposite. Rejoin the road again and turn left uphill on it. ▶ The route levels as the buildings of Les Pradels come into view.

Leave the road before entering the hamlet by taking a wide dirt track off to the right (GR70 and Sentier de la Bête (!) waymark), soon passing water troughs. Climb on this track for about 500 metres to a signpost banning cars and motorcycles. Here bear left onto another track which heads eastwards. The trail skirts the edge of woodland to reach a cinder track at a noticeboard for the Forêt Domaniale de Mercoire. Turn right along this track, still following the edge of woodland. After about 500 metres, before reaching **Lac de Louradou**, turn left onto a grassy track at a GR70 signpost. This leads to the lake where there is a large wooden shelter and picnic tables.

There are good views looking back and to the left over the gentle wooden hills of the region.

Bear left, with the lake on your right, to begin an ancient, medieval route to Luc (a signpost here indicates that it is 3.5km to the Château de Luc). Cross a wooden footbridge and bear left on the Promenade de l'Abiouradou. Climb through the trees to reach a gravel track where you turn left. After about 100 metres leave the Sentier de la Bête, which bears left, but walk ahead on an earthen track signposted to Luc and La Bastide. Soon leave the Promenade de l'Abiouradou, which goes of to the right, but remain ahead following the sign for the Château de Luc, 2.7km.

The trail comes out onto a surfaced forest road – go ahead on this. When this road swings sharply to the left, ignore a track off to the right, but 25 metres later take a footpath on the right (the numbers 12 and 10 should be seen on a nearby tree) along the edge of woodland. There are glorious views from here of the approaching hills of the Cévennes. Cross a road and continue down-hill on a path, the Sentier de Liaison.

On the Sentier de Liaison

The trail drops steeply on an ancient rocky path down into the valley below. Cross the modern road again, which because of vehicular traffic has to take many hairpin bends, and continue downhill on the old mule track through the trees. On this descent you will get your first view of the Madonna and château over to your left. When you reach the road again, cross it, following the signpost to the 12th-century Château de Luc, with the 'tall white statue of Our Lady'.

After a visit to the ruins of the château (which have been much restored since my first visit in 1988), bear right on the path in front of its entrance. Descend to **Luc**, ⓘ turning right on reaching a road in the village, straight over a crossroads and walk towards the church and war memorial (water fountain here). Follow the C2 minor road, passing a modern Calvary, the cemetery and a metal crucifix before reaching a main road, the D906. Walk ahead on this road, until after about 800 metres bear left off the D906 to enter the hamlet of **Pranlac**, taking a level

Château de Luc

Bridge over the River Allier at Pranlac

crossing over the railway line. Walk through the hamlet on the D76 to cross the old bridge over the River Allier, so leaving Pranlac and the Lozère and entering the village of **Laveyrune** and the Ardèche.

Walk through the sprawling village on the D154, ignoring a road off to the left at a stone cross and the *mairie*, following the Allier to reach Laveyrune church. Remain on the D154 after leaving the village behind, climbing past a huge pylon. About a kilometre after Laveyrune church leave the road by turning left onto an earthen track at a Chemin de Stevenson signpost. ⓘ This track soon descends, passes a picnic table and reaches the outskirts of the small village of **Rogleton**. Cross a road, bearing left on another lane that descends to cross a stream and then climbs to a track junction.

The GR70 goes off to the right here to reach La Bastide in 3km, but we continue ahead, uphill, following the *GR de pays* (red-and-yellow waymarks) sign for the Abbaye N. D. des Neiges. Climb on this surfaced lane to where it levels. Here bear right on a stony track (red-and-yellow waymark), climbing steeply through woodland, zigzagging and passing under high-tension electricity cables, then following their general direction east-south-east uphill. Still following the red-and-yellow waymarks, ignore a path off to the right. Continue to ignore any side turnings, following the high-tension electricity cables up to the highest point (1225m), where there is a huge pylon and a small IGN triangulation survey point.

After admiring the fine view from here ('...I beheld suddenly a fine, wild landscape to the south. High rocky hills, blue as amethyst...') continue ahead, heading eastwards (magnetic bearing 85 degrees). Keep to the main track, ignoring side turnings, until after about 800 metres you reach a small clearing in the forest. At this point bear off to the right on a descending grassy track, magnetic bearing 160 degrees. The start of this track should be marked with a small metal sign indicating N. D. des Neiges, which should be on the right-hand side of the track about 15 metres in from the main track, and also by a single green paint stripe on a tree on the left side of the beginning of the grassy track.

Having located the start of the track, head downhill along it, passing under high-tension electricity cables. A little later ignore a track off to the left, but keep ahead, still on a magnetic bearing of 160 degrees, down the track. When you reach a track T-junction, turn left downhill, magnetic bearing 50 degrees. Within 150 metres you will arrive at a narrow metalled lane. Turn right, downhill, on this, soon reaching the monastery complex of **Notre-Dame-des-Neiges**. ⓘ

After a visit to the monastery locate a GR7 signpost indicating the way to La Bastide. This will be found just below the church. Head southwestwards on a surfaced track. After a little over a kilometre do not turn left to cross the river, but turn right at a T-junction where there should be a sign for Les Bories. Just before a large solitary house, turn right onto a dirt track, so passing to the right of the house (i.e. Les Bories).

At a T-junction of tracks by a pine wood, bear left and follow the track to pass a house on the left and meet a small road at a bend. Turn left on this lane, but after a

Monastery buildings and farm, Notre-Dame-des-Neiges

few hundred metres leave it for a narrow trod descending on the right. Emerge at the first houses of **La Bastide**, bearing left downhill into the village and continue on to the church at its centre.

POINTS OF INTEREST

Stevenson Information Boards
From time to time in the Département of Lozère, large and attractive information boards will be encountered along the RLS Trail, notably at Langogne, Sagne-Rousse and the Château de Luc. These boards give details of Stevenson's journey relevant to the particular area where they are located.

Luc
The main item of interest is the massive white Madonna at the ruins of the fortified castle on the hill overlooking the town and valley of the Allier. It is 4m high and was

Stevenson interpretation board at Luc

dedicated, as Stevenson noted, on 6 October 1878, less than two weeks after his visit. RLS was told that the statue weighed 50 quintals. A dictionary definition of a quintal is a hundredweight, which can be either 112lb or 100lb. However, a quintal *metrique*, or French quintal, equals 100kg, which is equivalent to 220lb avoirdupois. Therefore 50 quintals can either be 5000lb, 5600lb or 11,000lb!

Since my first visit in 1988 the ruins of Château de Luc have been much restored by the Friends of Luc Castle ('Les Amis de Château de Luc'). The main tower (donjon) has been appreciably restored and is open to the public every day in the summer season from 3pm until 7pm (small entrance charge). The Château de Luc was an important place on one of France's medieval pilgrimage routes, as Saint Gilles (the Guardian of the pilgrim route of Régordane) lived here. Luc was a strategic location between the ancient provinces of Gévaudan and Vivarais.

Monastery of Notre-Dame-des-Neiges ('Our Lady of the Snows')

The present monastery complex dates from after 1912, when the buildings visited by RLS were destroyed by fire. Not only the fabric, but also the activities and way of life of the Trappist monks have changed enormously since the 1870s. No longer confined to a life of silence, the monks are now astute businessmen, selling wine, honey, cheeses and souvenirs to the hordes of tourists who are daily disgorged from fleets of tour coaches during the summer season. There are wine cellars to visit, an excellent audio-visual display (20 minutes duration and free to visitors) on the history of the monastery and the life and work of the inhabitants, a café and, of course, a number of services in the abbey that the public are welcome to attend. The single austere rooms for travellers found in Stevenson's day have been replaced by plush accommodation, mainly used by relatives and friends of the monks, and by others for spiritual retreats.

There is a common misconception, found in some books on the region, and even told by the present-day monks, that RLS spent three days at Notre-Dame-des-Neiges. He in fact spent only one night there, Thursday 26 September 1878, but lunched with the monks the following day before leaving for La Bastide and Chasseradés.

STAGE 7 – *La Bastide-Puylaurent to Les Alpiers or Le Bleymard*

26.1km (16.2 miles) or 28km (17.4 miles)
7hrs 20mins or 7hrs 55mins

Location	Distance (km)		Time (hr min)	
	Section	Cum	Section	Cum
La Bastide-Puylaurent (1016m)	0.0	0.0	0 00	0 00
Chabalîer	9.7	9.7	2 35	2 35
Chasseradès	2.2	11.9	0 35	3 10
Mirandol	1.2	13.1	0 30	3 40
L'Estampe	1.4	14.5	0 30	4 10
Serreméjan	5.4	19.9	1 30	5 40
Les Alpiers (1186m)	6.2	26.1	1 40	7 20
Le Bleymard (La Remise) (1069m)	1.9	28.0	0 35	7 55

The days begins with a morning's walk over the high country to the north of the Allier valley, crossing the watershed of France before descending once more into this valley to meet and follow the line of the railway, through the villages of Chasseradès and Mirandol. Stevenson met some of the workmen surveying this countryside in preparation for the coming railway, which happily is still in operation today. The monumental Mirandol railway viaduct is passed en route for the hamlet of L'Estampe, which in 1988 housed the first *gîte d'étape* since Goudet back in Stage 1! Sadly, this rustic hostel has now closed its doors, but the building still stands proudly in the village.

The route continues with a crossing of the Goulet range of hills before a lengthy detour down through woodland to visit the deserted hamlet of Serreméjan. The source of the Lot, one of southern France's principle rivers, is encountered before a descent is made to the tourist town of Le Bleymard, on the very edge of the Cévennes. This is quite a long day's walk, the longest and hardest so far, but can be shortened a little by an overnight stay in the *gîte d'étape* above the hamlet of Les Alpiers.

FACILITIES

The shop in Chasseradès closed in 2006. There is a trendy bar and two-star hotel/restaurant in the centre of the village, and another hotel/restaurant is passed just a little before the village, with a *camping à la ferme* some way before this (see Route).

Mirandol has a *gîte d'étape*, but no shop or café. Note that the *gîte d'étape* in L'Estampe is now closed, despite the fact that some old signposts indicate its existence.

There are no opportunities for refreshment between Mirandol and Les Alpiers, which has only a *gîte d'étape*. All facilities will be found in Le Bleymard, including a municipal campsite (La Gazelle), *chambres d'hôte* and a hotel in La Remise, which serves superb French and Lozère cuisine. There are shops, a large supermarket, a bar, *boulangerie*, post office and *office de tourisme* all in the village.

Mirandol gîte d'étape

TRAVELS WITH A DONKEY

After his night in a cell in the monastery of Notre-Dame-des-Neiges, Stevenson delayed his departure the next day, discussing politics and, even more unwisely, religion, with some of the boarders there. Eventually he was escorted back towards La Bastide by his Irish friend, Michael O'Callaghan (Travels with a Donkey, Stage 6), and from there continued along the Allier to Chasseradès, 'a tumbled village on a water course in a bare valley between two bare ranges of hills', where he arrived at sunset. He stayed the night at the village inn with five other guests, all of whom were 'employed in survey for one of the projected railroads'. Politics were discussed until a late hour, when all retired to one stifling room containing four beds. Stevenson, being a gentleman, was allowed a bed to himself.

RLS was woken at the inn in Chasseradès at daybreak, which in those days was 5am (France was not on western European summer time, so dawn came much earlier than it does in late September in the 21st century). He was soon on his way to L'Estampe, and from there climbed to the southwest over the Montagne du Goulet. He was in good spirits, believing that he was '…now done with rains and winds and a bleak country'.

This was a significant point on his journey. He was now, at long last, entering the Cévennes. 'The first part of my journey ended here; and this was like an induction of sweet sounds into the other and more beautiful.' On 'springy and well scented' turf, and with no 'company but a lark or two', he descended into the shallow valley of the Lot, beyond which he observed the range of the Lozère, 'sparsely wooded and well enough modelled in the flanks, but straight and dull in outline'.

ROUTE

At the church in **La Bastide**, bear right, west-northwest, to cross the bridge over the River Allier, then bear right to follow the sign to La Gare. Cross the railway line at the official crossing point just after the station building and climb the hill on the other side, signposted as the GR7

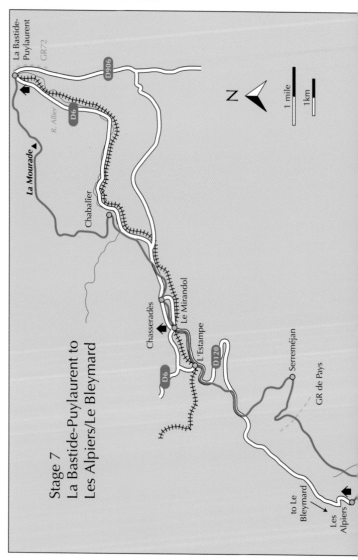

Stage 7
La Bastide-Puylaurent to
Les Alpiers/Le Bleymard

and GR7A, but after a few metres reach the point where these two GR trails and the GR70 part company. Follow the GR70 signpost uphill, indicating Chasseradès in 3 hours and Le Bleymard in 8 hours on the Chemin de Mercoire (the GR7 to Belvézet – 5 hours – and to Le Bleymard – 8 hours – goes off to the right).

The surfaced lane soon becomes a dirt track as it enters woodland. It climbs to the southwest, and where it turns to head northwest campers should turn off to the left, following a signpost for the campsite (in 1.9km). But remain on the good track for the RLS Trail, as it later swings left to head southwest again, climbing for the first time above 1300m to reach the summit of **La Mourade** (1308m). ▶ There is a good all-round view from here, with the high mountains of the Cévennes now beckoning ahead.

A little before the highest point you will pass a picnic area with picnic tables and a wooden hitching post for your donkey!

After La Mourade continue west-southwestwards over the Plateau de la Gardille (aka the Plateau du Chambonnet), ignoring any side tracks for over 2km to approach the Rocher de la Réchaubo. On meeting another track at a bend, bear left and 100 metres later ignore another track on the left, soon passing a notice-board indicating that you are entering the Forêt Domaniale de la Gardille. Continue to a major cross-tracks about 150 metres to the east of the Rocher de la Réchaubo (1319m), where the trail turns left. Follow the signpost to Chabalîer (2.1km), now heading south and descending on an earthen track.

The trail eventually bends to the east to enter the hamlet of **Chabalîer**. Bear right on the road descending past the houses. ▶ Turn right at a small stone cross on the left, continuing the descent into the valley. Cross a bridge over the Allier, which is only a small stream at this point, and 6 metres before a 'stop' sign for the main D6, bear right onto an earthen track. Soon ford a stream (the Ruisseau de Fontaleyres) and continue on this trail, later ignoring a track on the right at an ancient, lichen-encrusted stone cross.

Note the large Stevenson 'scare-crow' with wooden donkey(!) on the left, indicating the way ahead.

On reaching a tarmacked lane, campers could opt for *camping à la ferme* by turning to the right for 200

Scarecrow Stevenson and Modestine, Chabalier

metres, but the RLS Trail turns left here to reach Chasseradès railway station (a request halt only), which is a kilometre east-northeast of the actual village. Turn right at a road T-junction. Later ignore the road off to the left to Grossefage and the municipal campsite in 800 metres, but remain on the D6, direction Mende, until you finally turn right to enter **Chasseradès**. ①

At the L'Elixer bar and hotel in the centre of the village, turn right up a gravel track and then left to reach the village church. Turn left in front of the church, following the waymark for the GR70, L'Estampe, and the *gîte d'étape* Le Mirandol in 1km. Pass to the right of the cemetery (tall stone cross on the right) and descend to the railway line, noting both the Mirandol viaduct ahead and the special tunnels that protect the railway line from snow in winter. Walk down through the hamlet of **Mirandol**, ① with its impressive gorge on the left, under a road bridge and then under the enormous railway viaduct. Cross a bridge over the river and ascend the lane ahead, leaving Mirandol to head for L'Estampe. ◀

At the top of a short climb turn right over rock slabs and in a few metres bear left. Ascend on a sunken path to

Note that this route from Mirandol to L'Estampe is not shown on the 1:25,000 IGN map, but is clear and easy to follow.

Viaduct at Mirandol

reach cross-tracks where you turn right, descend, cross a small stream and re-ascend with the railway line over to the right. Reach and follow the railway line to a lane in **L'Estampe**. ① At L'Estampe RLS encountered huge numbers of sheep: 'The narrow street of Estampe was full of sheep, black and white all bleating and tinkling the bells around their necks.' ▶

Bear left on the narrow village road, passing the old *gîte d'étape* on the right, and leave L'Estampe on the D120, climbing gently with views to the wooded mountains ahead, and beginning the ascent of the **Goulet** massif. ① The road bends as it climbs, but about 100 metres before it enters trees, turn right on a track which itself soon reaches trees. Fifty metres after entering the trees bear left at a Y-junction and 50 metres later take the right, lower fork. A hundred metres afterwards at another Y-junction take the left fork, climbing. Now keep to this old main track ascending steeply through the wood, ignoring minor tracks to left and right. The track eventually swings sharply to the left and continues to rejoin the D120.

Turn right on the D120, continuing the climb up to a col at 1413m. Here locate a memorial stone to a forester,

In 1988, the first *gîte d'étape* on the RLS Trail since Goudet on the first day was located here in L'Estampe, although it has now closed.

123

Guy Cubizolle. Turn left at this point, making sure the memorial stone is on your left, to follow a stony earthen track (GR70 waymark) that gradually descends through woodland. Ignore minor tracks to left and right. At a major track Y-junction take the right-hand fork heading downhill. Later ignore a track off to the left. Continue the long descent, eventually reaching another track at a bend. Turn sharply to the right here to reach the ruins of the abandoned hamlet of **Serreméjan**, ⓘ a very sad sight. After the last building be sure to take the left fork at a Y-junction of tracks (no waymark here in 2006).

Cross a stream (usually dry) and continue now steeply uphill. At a hairpin bend ignore the descending track left, but turn right, ascending gradually. At a second hairpin bend turn sharply to the left, still ascending. Eventually you will reach a major cross-tracks. This is an ancient drove road, La Draille des Mulets. Turn right here for 15 metres and then left down a grassy track. This soon becomes an eroded path, which descends steeply to the source of the **River Lot**, ⓘ one of southern France's major rivers.

Descending through the woods to Les Alpiers

The path becomes a grassy track. At a junction of tracks it is important to take the right fork (it should be well waymarked), continuing the descent. Turn right (north) at a track T-junction. The trail swings to the left at a GR70 signpost (there should also be a sign here indicating the way to La Boulaie *gîte d'étape* in Les Alpiers). The path descends to the left of a barbed-wire fence, with the stream of the nascent Lot trickling down on your right.

Emerge onto a track where you continue ahead, downhill. Cross the stream and continue with the infant Lot now on your left, climbing a little to reach a track T-junction at the edge of a pine forest. Turn right and continue along this track to a road. Turn right here for 300 metres to reach the *gîte d'étape* – it is the large house that is visible from the track/road junction – but to reach **Les Alpiers** ⓘ hamlet itself turn left along the road for 300 metres.

Walk down through the hamlet to take an earthen track that starts where the tarmac ends by an ancient, primitive stone crucifix. When the track divides take the left-hand fork, with the village of Le Bleymard seen in the valley below. Descend to reach the main road, the D901, at La Remise, a 'suburb' of Le Bleymard. Campers should turn left for 100 metres, if staying at the municipal campsite, but others turn right to enter **Le Bleymard**. ⓘ The Hôtel La Remise is a few hundred metres on the right, just after a large supermarket on the left.

POINTS OF INTEREST

Watershed

The elevated land between La Bastide and Chasseradès is one of the principal watersheds of Europe. The Allier flows from one side of it, into the Loire at Nevers and on into the Atlantic, while the Chassezac, the stream that runs through Chasseradès, will eventually join the Rhône and head for the Mediterranean. The head springs of the Allier and the Chassezac lie a mere 150 metres or so apart.

The church at Chasseradès

Chasseradès

The 12th-century Romanesque church in this authentic Lozère village, built of rough-hewn stone, is worthy of a visit.

Mirandol

The massive curving railway viaduct dominates the view. It is 120 metres long and stands 30 metres over the Chassezac river. This, and the remainder of the line to Mende, was being surveyed at the time of Stevenson's visit. Notice the slate tiles *(lauzes)* on the roofs of the houses in the village.

L'Estampe

Note the swallowhole beside the road just above the hamlet (marked Gfre, for 'Gouffre', on the IGN map). There are many more swallowholes on the limestone plateau of the Causse de Montbelle above Belvézet, to the northwest of L'Estampe.

Le Goulet (1497m/4908ft)

The first major climb of the walk and the start of the Cévennes mountains. Once out of the trees on the descent, the views are extensive. The RLS Trail reaches a high point of 1413m, but the actual summit (viewpoint) can be reached by following a *GR de pays* detour of about 2.4 km to the west.

Serreméjan

The sad fate of this hamlet is typical of so many other peasant communities in southern France, where employment opportunities in the towns caused a drifting away from the countryside during the 19th and 20th centuries, as the simple but hard and primitive rustic life of isolated rural areas became untenable.

Ancient crucifix, Les Alpiers

Les Alpiers

This hamlet too has seen the effects of depopulation. Things have improved since my last visit in the late 1980s, although several of the smarter properties here are now holiday homes. Note the small, ancient primitive cross by the roadside.

Le Bleymard

This pleasant town, which has a number of interesting old houses, is now a thriving ski resort, owing its popularity to the vicinity of Mont Lozère, ideal for both downhill and cross-country *ski de fond*. In June there is an annual 'Festival Stevenson' in Le Bleymard and in the Mont Lozère area, lasting for three days.

River Lot

The trail crosses the River Lot at Le Bleymard, only a few kilometres from its source in the foothills of the Cévennes, to the northeast of Les Alpiers.

STAGE 8 – Les Alpiers or Le Bleymard to Le Pont-de-Montvert

21.1km (13.1 miles) or 19.2km (11.9 miles)
6hrs 35mins or 6hrs

Location	Distance (km)		Time (hr min)	
	Section	Cum	Section	Cum
Les Alpiers (1186m)	0.0	0.0	0 00	0 00
Le Bleymard (La Remise) (1069m)	1.9	1.9	0 35	0 35
Col Santel (1200m)	2.0	3.9	0 45	1 20
Chalet du Mont Lozère	2.7	6.6	1 00	2 20
Pic de Finiels (1699m)	4.3	10.9	1 25	3 45
Finiels	4.8	15.7	1 15	5 00
Le Pont-de-Montvert (875m)	5.4	21.1	1 35	6 35

Lovers of mountain country will find much to their liking today as the trail makes a traverse of the Mont Lozère massif, reaching the highest point not only of the trail, but also in the whole of the Cévennes, the Pic de Finiels at 1699m (5570ft). The ascent is a gradual one, never too steep, and route finding in clear conditions is not a problem, as much of the way on the mountainside is marked with montjoies, ancient, tall granite marker posts. But in adverse weather the situation would be very different, and it would be prudent to either take the lower and easier alternative route via the Col de Finiels, or wait in Le Bleymard or at the Chalet du Mont Lozère complex until conditions improve. Do try to make an early start today in order to arrive in Le Pont-de-Montvert in the early afternoon, to allow sufficient time to enjoy this delightful mountain village. There will be no time for this tomorrow morning!

FACILITIES
The Mont Lozère complex (Station du Mont Lozère) consists of two hotel/restaurants and a *gîte d'étape*. Drinks are also available here. Between the Station du Mont

Stone shelter on the descent to Finiels

Lozère and Finiels, the only shelter to be had in bad weather is the small *abri* (cabin) passed en route south of the Pic de Finiels. Like a Scottish bothy it is always left open for use by walkers and other passing travellers. **Note that wild camping is not allowed in the Cévennes National Park.**

There is a *chambre d'hôte* in the tiny village of Finiels. Limited food, such as local cheese, jam and apple juice, may be on sale from some of the farmsteads in the village, but there is no *épicerie*.

Le Pont-de-Montvert has accommodation of all types. There are two good hotels, a fine *gîte d'étape communal* housed in the Ecomuseum building complex, and a campsite down by the River Tarn. Plentiful shops, supermarkets, a *boulangerie*, restaurants, cafés and bars are to be found in the village, as well as a post office, bank, and tourist office with a Cévennes National Park information centre.

TRAVELS WITH A DONKEY

Stevenson lunched in Le Bleymard before goading Modestine up through the woods towards Mont Lozère, where he found a 'dell of green turf, where a streamlet made a little spout over some stones to serve me for a water-tap'. Here he spent, 'A Night Among the Pines', greatly enjoying the scents, sounds and sights of a starry night on the mountain. Although delighting in his own company he was obviously missing Fanny Osbourne, for he wrote, 'to live out of doors with a woman a man loves is of all lives the most complete and free'. He was to write later that *Travels with a Donkey* was full of 'mere protestations to F'. He so enjoyed the night in the open air that he decided to leave some payment, '...to leave pieces of money on the turf as I went along, until I had left enough for my night's lodging'.

Stevenson was in high spirits during the morning he spent on Mont Lozère, enjoying the sunshine and extensive views of the high Cévennes. On reaching the highest point on his entire journey on the Pic de Finiels, he was moved by the 'confused and shaggy country' at his feet and the 'undecipherable labyrinth of hills', declaring that these are 'the Cévennes of the Cévennes'.

One of the reasons for his journey was to visit the land of the Camisards, the French equivalent of the Scottish Covenanters, and on crossing the Lozère he wrote that he '...had travelled through a dull district...', but that now he '...was to go down into the scene of a romantic chapter...in the history of the world'.

RLS followed a line of *montjoies* (ancient marker stones) to the top of the Pic de Finiels, and then a track corkscrewing 'into a valley between falling hills, stubbly with rocks like a reaped field of corn, and floored further down with green meadows'. He descended quickly, 'The whole descent is like a dream to me, so rapidly was it accomplished', seeing 'not a human creature' until 'the Tarn at Pont de Montvert of bloody memory...The place, with its houses, its lanes, its glaring river bed, wore an indescribable air of the South.'

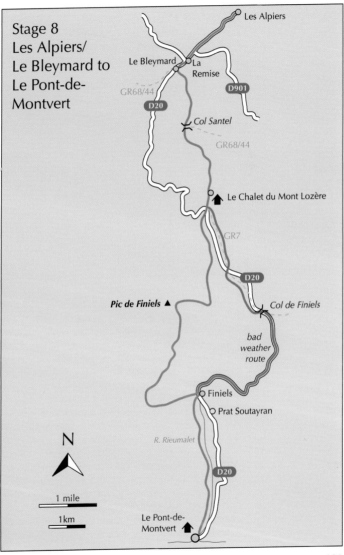

Stage 8
Les Alpiers/
Le Bleymard to
Le Pont-de-
Montvert

Les Alpiers

Le Bleymard La Remise

GR68/44

D901

D20

Col Santel

GR68/44

Le Chalet du Mont Lozère

GR7

D20

Pic de Finiels ▲

Col de Finiels

*bad
weather
route*

Finiels

Prat Soutayran

R. Rieumalet

D20

N

1 mile

1km

Le Pont-de-
Montvert

Looking back to Les Alpiers

ROUTE

Those staying at the *gîte d'étape* in Les Alpiers must first walk to **La Remise**. The way is described in the last paragraph of the route, Stage 7.

From La Remise turn left off the main road, sign-posted **Le Bleymard**, D20. In about 250 metres, at the monument to Henri Rouvière (a French anatomist), turn left on the Rue de Couderc. (Those wanting the bar, *boulangerie* or *office de tourisme*, or a visit to the church and centre of Le Bleymard village, should keep ahead at the monument, on the Rue Principale.)

At the top of the small hill, take the left of three minor roads. At a small metal cross and concrete bench at a bend in the road, turn right on a track, the old *draille* (drove road). ◄ In about 50 metres ignore the upper path that veers off to the left, but keep ahead with buildings below right. Climb this grassy track, descend slightly to a T-junction at a sandy track, and turn right, continuing to **Col Santel**.

Note that alternatively you can reach this point by following the yellow and green Chemin de Stevenson signs through the village.

At Col Santel there is a division of paths. Left leaves on the GR44/68 to Cubières in 45 minutes, but ahead lies the GR7, coincident with the GR70, signposted to Le **Mont Lozère**. ① Climb through the forest, heading for the mast seen ahead. After a few hundred metres of climbing remain on the main track as it bears left. This stony track climbs steeply through the woods. Follow a 'pine tree' waymark and red-and-white paint stripes at path junctions to emerge from the trees, with the hills and ridges of the Cévennes stretching ahead into the distance. The track now descends slightly before gradually re-ascending to the D20 at the **Chalet du Mont Lozère**.

The unattractive complex here has a number of buildings: a *station de ski*, chalets, bar/restaurant with combined *gîte d'étape* (Le Refuge), and a two-star hotel and bar/restaurant opposite – the Chalet du Mont Lozère itself. An information office of the Parc National des Cévennes is also located here (open in main seasons only).

Continue past the complex (ignoring the GR7, which takes a sandy track on the left – see Bad Weather Alternative at the end of this route description), remaining on the D20 to pass a modern chapel on the right, and encountering the first of many *montjoies* (tall granite waymarker standing stones).

Pick up a thin path on the right-hand side of the road following a low wooden fence. Reach a signpost indicating the direction to Le Pont-de-Montvert in 10km. At this point follow the path, which now pulls away from the road, through heather and scattered pine trees and bushes. This ancient **draille** ① (drove road) up the hillside is a good and clear one, and is also well waymarked with *montjoies*, many of which have been re-erected in modern times to mark the route of the GR70.

The pines eventually thin out to leave a bare hillside strewn with heather and low *myrtille* (bilberry) bushes. ▸ As the route is so well waymarked with *montjoies*, it can be safely followed even in mist (I can testify to this!), although in such conditions those who prefer an easier and safer route to Finiels should follow the Bad Weather

Note that it is prohibited to pick *myrtille* berries in this conservation area of the national park.

133

Alternative described at the end of this route description, which goes via the **Col de Finiels** rather than the Pic de Finiels.

The trail leads southwards to a shallow saddle at a signpost. The line of *montjoies* continues to the south, but the RLS Trail turns sharply to the west here, to follow a line of tall wooden 'snow poles', leading in about a kilometre from the saddle to the summit of Mont Lozère, the **Pic de Finiels**.

After the saddle, the first top is a minor one where there is a small stone shelter. From this top, the continuing trail becomes indistinct on the ground, and in mist the route is a little tricky. Follow a magnetic compass bearing of 260 degrees to climb to another stone shelter, this time on the summit of the Pic de Finiels (1699m), the highest point in the Cévennes and also on the RLS Trail. On the flat summit you will find a small IGN triangulation survey point, and most likely the word 'Finiels' spelt out in stones.

Descend due south on a grassy sward for about 400 metres to a track T-junction. Turn left here, following the edge of pine bushes for about 150 metres, where a large cairn and waymarks indicate a turn to the right. Descend steeply southwards on a rough stone track through bushes, which later give way to trees. On reaching a track T-junction turn right for 50 metres to a wider track, where you turn left to pass a small *abri*, or primitive shelter, which would be a godsend in bad weather. If you do enter, be sure to take all your litter away with you, and to fasten the door securely to prevent animals getting in and despoiling the cabin.

Follow the main forest track as it bends to the right. Ignore other trails, keeping to this main track until, about a kilometre after the *abri*, turn right at a track junction onto a narrower track through the trees. On reaching the edge of the trees, turn left onto a track that descends with the wood on your left. When the trees end, continue ahead over open country on a stony track enclosed by barbed-wire fences. At a track junction after a few hundred metres, it is important that you take

The hamlet of Finiels

the track descending eastwards, to the left. The hamlet of **Finiels** ⓘ is soon seen below, and is reached in about 1.2km of walking.

On reaching the road at a bend on the outskirts of Finiels, bear right on it, downhill. At the road sign for Finiels, turn right off the road to descend, passing a water fountain and an old *métier à vache* (see Preyssac, Points of Interest, Stage 2). Continue ahead on a surfaced track to pass to the right of a tiny cemetery. Remain on this track as it leaves the village, heading southwards.

At a junction take a left fork to head down the valley, walking through areas of **chaos** ⓘ boulders. The trail narrows to a footpath through the boulders. Pass through a wooden gate and continue the descent on the footpath. The route becomes steep and eroded and leads to a gate and wooden footbridge. Cross this to follow the enclosed path above and to the right of the river.

This path eventually descends to a path junction where the GR70 goes to the left, down to the river at a

135

ford. If it is safe, cross this and follow the path that leads to the D20, which takes you down into the valley. In times of flood (*par temps de crue*), however, turn right, uphill, at the path junction (see above, where the GR70 goes to the left). This variant route avoids the river crossing at the ford (which can be very deep when the river is high, as I can testify!), climbing instead to reach a tarmacked lane. Turn left on this lane to descend to cross the river by a road bridge. The lane leads to the D20, where you turn right, back on the main trail.

About 400 metres along the D20, where the road begins to bend to the left, leave it to take a footpath on the right, which leads to a large glass sliding door! This is an entrance to the Ecomuseum. Pass through the door (it is always unlocked even when the museum is closed) to follow this ancient route into the village of **Le Pont-de-Montvert**. ⓘ The *gîte d'étape communal* is here, its entrance door immediately on the right. Walk ahead through the fascinating open building to emerge on a footpath that leads down to the centre of Le Pont-de-Montvert.

A view from the old bridge over the Tarn, Le Pont-de-Montvert

BAD WEATHER ALTERNATIVE

In conditions of low visibility, cloud, hill fog, heavy rain or snow, the following route to the hamlet of Finiels is recommended, via the Col de Finiels. This route follows the GR7 to the Col de Finiels, then takes the D20 down to Finiels village. The distance from the Chalet du Mont Lozère to Finiels by this route is 9.8km, which will occupy about 2 hours 30 minutes of walking.

From the complex of buildings on Mont Lozère, proceed to the D20 and turn left to enter the Parc National des Cévennes. In 75 metres bear left, just before a modern chapel on the right, onto a brown, surfaced road. Pass under a ski lift and climb on this road, which follows the line of the modern D20, but remains below it. After about 800 metres, bear left off this surfaced road onto a grassy track. This route is that of the old *draille* (drove road).

Pass under a *teleski* and in 20 metres bear right on the higher track. This soon becomes a narrow path with a fence on the left. This path eventually fords a stream and rejoins the road. Turn left and continue uphill on a path to the left of the road with a fence to the left. A little later cross over the road and take a stony track, now with the road over to the left. On joining the D20 again, continue uphill to the Col de Finiels, the highest point on the road at 1541m.

At the Col de Finiels ignore the track off to the left (the GR7), but instead remain on the D20. This winding road continues over the plateau until, on emerging from the woods, a glorious mountain panorama of rocky ridges and distant blue mountains opens out. There are a number of large boulders in a variety of curious formations to be seen close to the road in this area, and on the descent there is a good view of the Pic de Finiels with the hamlet of Finiels nestling below. Continue on the road until you enter Finiels, from where you follow the route described above to Le Pont-de-Montvert.

POINTS OF INTEREST

Mont Lozère

The Pic de Finiels (1699m/5570ft) and the alternative Col de Finiels (1541m/5055ft) on Mont Lozère are the highest points reached on the RLS Trail, and the only time that the 5000 feet mark is exceeded. The Pic de Finiels is the highest point on Mont Lozère and in the Cévennes – indeed, only the volcanic *puys* of Mont-Dore and Cantal in the Auvergne, and Mont Mézenc in the Velay, exceed it in height in the whole of the Massif Central. The view is extensive, with even the Mediterranean visible on a clear day.

Drailles (Drove Roads)

There are many ancient drailles in the Cévennes, but very few indeed are now used to drive sheep or cattle along to market. These old tracks often provide the best and easiest walking through the rugged, stony and scrub-covered hills. The RLS Trail uses many of them on its way south to Saint-Jean-du-Gard. *Drailles* are particularly evident on Mont Lozère, where they are often marked with a line of *montjoies* (standing stones) dating from the old droving days. Ancient boundary stones engraved with Maltese crosses may also be found on the ridges of Mont Lozère.

Granite montjoie marking the route

Chaos

On the descent from the Col or Pic de Finiels to the village of the same name, several large piles of granite blocks and boulders will be seen. These are called *chaos* in French, and are a particular, and very photogenic, feature of the southern slopes of the Mont Lozère massif.

Finiels

An annual 'Fete of the Myrtilles' (bilberries) is held in August in this small mountain village. Note also the old *métier à vache* in the village (see Preyssac, Points of Interest, Stage 2).

Le Pont-de-Montvert

A most picturesque Cévenol village located at the confluence of three rivers, the Tarn, Rieumalet and Martinet. There are many fine 16th-century houses built along narrow winding streets on rocks above the waters, but possibly the most attractive feature of the village is the 17th-century humpbacked bridge over the River Tarn. (The Cévennes National Park information centre is no longer housed in the old toll tower on this bridge, but is now in a small, purpose-built building on the river's edge in the main street of the village.) Another building of interest is the Protestant Temple. Now tranquil, it bears witness to far more troubled earlier times (see below).

The Écomusée du Lozère (ecological museum) is built over the ancient path into the village, and houses some most interesting displays, on subjects such as the environment of the uplands and the harsh rural life of bygone centuries (open during the main summer months; small entrance fee). Finally of interest to RLS Trail walkers will be the headquarters of the Association Sur Le Chemin de Robert Louis Stevenson (see Appendix 5), located in a building a few houses along from the *mairie*. The staff will no doubt be delighted to see satisfied customers if you wish to pay them a brief visit.

It was in Le Pont-de-Montvert in 1702 that the War of the Camisards broke out. Events leading to this particularly vicious and bloody struggle for religious freedom

Old houses in Le Pont-de-Montvert

began in 1589 with the issuing of the Edict of Nantes by Henry IV of France. The edict granted religious toleration to French Protestants, but was revoked in 1685 by Louis XIV, with the practice of the austere Protestant faith being forbidden by the Catholic authorities. As a result, some 400,000 French Protestants (Huguenots) fled the country for more religiously tolerant states in northern Europe; many settled in Britain.

Although many left from the Cévennes, these were hard mountain people who resisted the attempt of the state to rid the area of Protestantism and force the alien Catholic faith on the population. Local representatives of the Catholic authorities, together with troops billeted on the residents, were used to coerce the population into Catholicism. Protestantism was practised in secret, usually in caves or fields, and most of the pastors went into hiding, continuing to preach and baptising, marrying and burying the dead in secret.

The Catholic authorities were responsible for many atrocities, and torture, imprisonment, deportation and execution were commonplace. The Catholic governor of the district around Le Pont-de-Montvert was the Abbé (or Archpriest) du Chayla, notorious for personally torturing Protestant prisoners, who he kept in the cellars of his riverside house. This house is no longer there, having been rebuilt as a grocers/souvenir shop, but the cellars can still be seen.

On the night of 24 July 1702, the Abbé du Chayla was brutally murdered at Le Pont-de-Montvert by a gang of 52 men, this event sparking off the guerrilla War of the Camisards, which continued for much of the ensuing century until the Revolutionary Government of 1789 granted religious freedom to French Protestants. Pierre-Esprit Séguier, the leader of the gang, was caught within a few days and burnt alive on 12 August. Catholic churches were burnt and their priests murdered as the populace organised themselves into a small guerrilla army under the leadership of Rolland and Jean Cavalier. The Protestants became known as the Camisards after the shirts (*camisa* in the old Occitan tongue) that distinguished them from the French army, which was dressed in uniform and armour.

Fearful retribution followed, with the King's army burning hundreds of Cévenol villages and massacring the inhabitants. All this had a devastating effect on the landscape, still much in evidence today, with a low, scattered population living in small wall-enclosed villages. At the time of Stevenson's visit in 1878, the War of the Camisards was just within living memory.

The injustices went deep; even today there are separatist organisations, and slogans written in Occitan may occasionally be seen. When visiting the Protestant chapel and the Catholic church in Le Pont-de-Montvert, it is well to bear in mind the events of the 18th century in this once troubled region.

STAGE 9 – Le Pont-de-Montvert to Florac

27.3km (17 miles)
8hrs 45mins

Location	Distance (km)		Time (hr min)	
	Section	Cum	Section	Cum
Le Pont-de-Montvert (875m)	0.0	0.0	0 00	0 00
Cham de l'Hermet (1114m)	2.0	2.0	0 55	0 55
Col de la Planette (1292m)	5.1	7.1	1 50	2 45
Col du Sapet (1080m)	5.6	12.7	1 45	4 30
Junction of GR68/70	5.7	18.4	1 55	6 25
Pont de la Pontèse	4.0	22.4	1 05	7 30
Le Pont du Tarn	3.8	26.2	1 00	8 30
Florac (546m)	1.1	27.3	0 15	8 45

Of all the excellent walking on the RLS Trail, today's route has to be the *crème de la crème*, with views all day of the highest order. Ironically, it is the only long section of the route that was not walked by the great man himself, as Stevenson used the track along the valley to Florac, on what is now the metalled and busy D998. The modern trail thankfully takes to the hills to follow the long and high Bougès ridge that runs westwards for many kilometres, eventually descending to the valley of the Tarnon and to Florac, the capital of the Cévennes, at the foot of the mighty Causses plateau.

But before this spectacular ridge is reached there are other delights, particularly the climb out of the valley of the Tarn on the ancient cobbled *draille* from Le Pont-de-Montvert. On the negative side, today's walk is the longest on the entire route, so be sure to make an early start to enjoy it to the full. Flagging walkers have the option of taking the shorter GR68 into Florac at the end of the day, saving at least an hour of effort.

FACILITIES

There are no possibilities of obtaining refreshments along today's route, and once Le Pont-de-Montvert is left, it is necessary to be self-sufficient until the end of

Cabane à Bonnal, a welcome haven on the Bougès ridge

the day at Florac. A detour into the village of Bédouès, only a few kilometres before Florac, will locate a café and restaurant towards the end of the walk. The main possibility for accommodation before reaching Florac is to make a long detour and descent (with re-ascent the next day!) to the south off the Bougès ridge, to the *gîte d'étape* at the hamlet of Mijavols.

A detour of about 1.6km to the east of the Pont de la Pontèse, near the end of the day, leads to the village of Cocurès, where there is a hotel/restaurant. Campers are a little more fortunate in that they can stay at the campsite (Camping Chantemerle) at the Pont de la Pontèse below Bédouès, but again this is only a few kilometres before Florac. There is another campsite, Le Chon du Tarn, to the southwest of Bédouès, north of Florac.

If you are unfortunate enough to be caught out in bad weather on the ridge there is a good shelter, the Cabane à Bonnal, to the east of the Col du Sapet (water source nearby).

143

Florac has all the facilities one would expect of the largest town in the Cévennes, with plentiful shops of most types, including several supermarkets, banks, a post office and a tourist office, and of course several restaurants, cafés and bars. The town also has at least four hotels and two *gîtes d'étape*. The municipal campsite, La Tière, will be found by the river on the southern edge of the town.

TRAVELS WITH A DONKEY

RLS had lunch at the inn at 'Pont de Montvert, or 'Greenhill Bridge', where he ate in the company of three women and flirted with the waitress. He left the village on 'a new road…from Pont de Montvert to Florac by the valley of the Tarn, a smooth sandy ledge'. Today this is a metalled road, the busy D998. Stevenson's spirits were still high as he journeyed beneath the chestnut trees, '…from bays of shadow into promontories of afternoon sun'. A short way down the valley he sought out a small 'unpleasantly exposed' plateau above the road, to where he 'goaded and kicked the reluctant Modestine' and camped for the night. Stevenson was by now enjoying his nights out under the stars, in fine and warm weather, although on this occasion he was bothered by rats that made disturbing sounds, 'such a noise as a person would make scratching loudly with a finger nail'. He was thus less pleased with his lodgings than on the previous night on Mont Lozère, so this time declined 'to leave pieces of money on the turf', but nevertheless gave money to a beggar woman he met the following morning.

After his 'morning toilette in the water of the Tarn' he continued down the valley, making several acquaintances on the way, including a 'Plymouth Brother' with whom he discussed religion and accompanied to the hamlet of La Vernède, 'a humble place, with less than a dozen houses, and a Protestant chapel on a knoll'. He took breakfast at the inn where he discovered that the villagers '…were all Protestants – a fact which pleased me more than I should have expected'.

*Collegiate church of
Bédouès*

After resting awhile with these friendly and 'upright
and simple' folk, he continued his journey, visiting the
ruins of the Château de Miral and passing through
Cocurès, 'sitting among vineyards and green meadows
and orchards', followed by Bédouès, where he saw 'a
battlemented monastery long since disabled and turned
into a church'. And so he arrived in Florac, 'as perfect a
little town as one would desire to see...with an old castle, an alley of planes, many quaint street-corners, and a
live fountain welling from the hill'.

He spent the afternoon and night at an inn in the
town where he conversed with the locals and was given
advice on the route for the next (and last) stage of his
journey to Saint-Jean-du-Gard. He observed that
'Protestant and Catholic intermingled in a very easy
manner', but was 'surprised to see what a lively memory
still subsisted of the religious war'.

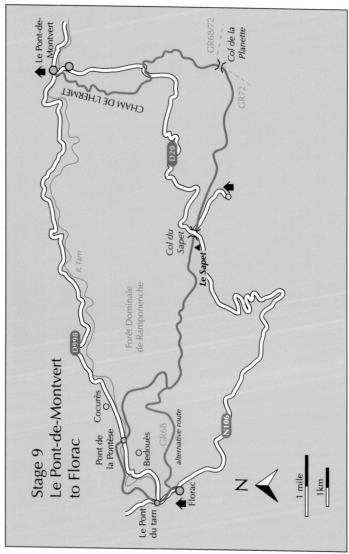

Stage 9
Le Pont-de-Montvert
to Florac

ROUTE

Cross the stone bridge over the River Tarn in the centre of **Le Pont-de-Montvert**, passing the old toll tower, and bear left for 10 metres until, when opposite the hotel Les Cévennes, turn right up a narrow street between houses (those requiring the campsite will find it by continuing ahead at this point, i.e. not making the right turn opposite the hotel). So begins a long steep climb up into the hills to the south of the village.

Climb steeply, pass through a wooden gate and leave the village by ascending an ancient cobbled footpath, once used by muleteers. This quite amazing path climbs steeply above the valley, offering fine views down to Le Pont-de-Montvert. The path passes through a couple of other gates to reach the plateau known as the **Cham de l'Hermet**. At the top of the climb be sure to look back. Your route from Mont Lozère and down the valley to Le Pont-de-Montvert is clearly visible. Say a last fond farewell to Le Pont-de-Montvert before turning your back on the scene and stepping out across the plateau on a good, narrow sandy footpath.

The path traverses the plateau for over a kilometre, widens to a sandy track and then descends a little. Before a road is reached be sure to turn left off the track onto a waymarked footpath, which heads southeastwards, enters trees and descends into the Fiarouze valley. Soon, after passing under power lines, the trail reaches the D20. Turn left here to cross the bridge over the river, and continue on this road for about 600 metres until you see a wide concrete track heading uphill on the right. Take this to climb steeply into the forest.

The concrete surface gives way to a sandy track as the trail levels to reach an open grassy area, the Champ Long de Bougès. Pass the farmstead of the same name and continue ahead at a cross-tracks signposted to Florac, again climbing steeply through the wood. On reaching a track junction continue ahead, still heading uphill. At a Y-junction of tracks keep to the right, on the lower of the two tracks, which continues the ascent to reach an open area, the **Col de la Planette** (1292m). ▶

At the Col de la Planette there is a memorial to Raymond Senn, who set up the GR68 and did much of the work developing the GR70, so RLS Trail walkers owe him a considerable debt.

The GR70 and **GR68** ⓘ   are coincident for the next 11km from this point, until the two part company nearly 6km west of the **Col du Sapet**.

Turn right at the Col de la Planette, heading westwards on a good track. After about 300 metres, at a small clearing (the Col des Trois Fayards) leave this track to bear right uphill, and 50 metres later turn left, climbing steeply on a path through the trees. Ascend to an unnamed summit at 1398m, crowned by a group of large 'stone men' cairns. Bear right here, descending to another col before climbing the Signal du Bougès, which at 1421m is both the highest point on the ridge and on today's route. The summit is marked by a large cairn and an IGN triangulation survey point, and the views are extensive – to the north to Mont Lozère, to the hills to the south and to the Causse in the west.

Continue westwards along the ridge, enjoying the spectacular views of the high Cévennes and the Causse. The ridge you are to follow stretches clearly out in front of you. Descend to the edge of trees, part of the huge Bois d'Altefage, where you ignore the track ahead, but instead bear left on a track that descends into the wood. Soon emerge from the trees again, and later pass the path that leads off to the left to Mijavols (in 3.5km).

After this junction you will soon arrive at a small wooden *abri* with a wooden picnic table outside and shelter and a table inside. This is the Cabane à Bonnal. A water source is located nearby (a description of how to find this should be pinned to the wall inside the cabin). Leave the hut to continue the descent on the rocky and sandy path, eventually reaching a road, the D20 again, at the Col du Sapet (1080m). Here there is a sign indicating that it is 10km to Florac on the GR68 but 12km on the GR70 – both figures are somewhat optimistic!

Cross the road to take the broad track westwards, to the north of **Le Sapet** (1114m) summit. Follow the main track, with good views out to the north to the Mont Lozère plateau, to enter the **Ramponenche Forest**. Remain on this forest track for several kilometres. Keep ahead on reaching a junction of seven tracks, slowly

Descending from the Signal de Bougès looking westwards to the Causses

descending through the wood, later passing a small stone shelter on the left and later still the small Reservoir de la Chaumette, again on the left. Soon after this reservoir the track swings to head north and then reaches an important track junction.

The shortest route into Florac is on the GR68, which turns to the left (see 'GR68 Alternative Route into Florac' below), but the RLS Trail, the GR70, remains on the main track as it swings sharply to the right to descend into the Ravin de Vallongue. After about a kilometre ignore a track off to the right, but instead swing to the left, continuing the descent. On reaching the **Tarn valley** ⓘ floor cross a ford and then follow the River Tarn, with a dramatic gorge down to your right. The track eventually climbs a little to a track junction at a bend. Bear right here to descend to a road to cross the Pont de la Pontèse over the River Tarn.

Immediately after crossing the bridge, turn left into Camping Chantemerle (two stars). At the end of the campsite ignore La Gardette on the right, but continue ahead at a 'No through road' sign, now following the opposite bank of the River Tarn. The lane becomes a footpath after passing a house on the right. The village of **Bédouès**, with its most impressive *collégiale* (collegiate church), is seen across the river to the south.

The footpath emerges onto a minor surfaced lane at another bridge over the Tarn. Continue ahead on this lane, still following the river. This minor road eventually becomes an unsurfaced track. Bear left at a junction. The trail climbs a little as it follows the course of the valley, which now swings towards the south. This ancient path passes between scores of *châtaigneraie* (chestnut trees), the fruits of which formed the staple diet of the populace in centuries past. ◀

Many, many more *châtaignerai*, for which the southern Cévennes is renowned, will be passed on your continuing route to Saint-Jean-du-Gard.

The path meets a road. Walk straight ahead, the GR70 now joining with the GR68 from La Fage, which has descended from the hill behind. Descend to a T-junction where you turn left to cross an old bridge and reach the main road, the N106. Bear left on this heading

Ariges château seen on the approach to Florac

south, keeping to the footpath on the right-hand side of the road. (Note the road sign informing that it is 73km from here to Alès by this main road.) After about 600 metres, opposite the point where the GR68 (the shorter alternative to Florac) comes out on the road on your left, turn right over the bridge, Pont de la Bessède, over the River Tarnon, so entering **Florac**, ⓘ the 'capital' of the Cévennes, and not far from the **Tarn gorges**. ⓘ

GR68 ALTERNATIVE INTO FLORAC

The GR68 allows those who are tired to shorten the long day from Le Pont-de-Montvert. From the GR68/GR70 junction it is 5km to Florac by the GR68, compared with the 8.9km of the GR70 route.

At a track junction where the GR70 goes off to the right, turn left to follow the GR68. Later, at a clearing where the track turns sharply to the left, look for a narrow path off to the right. The path descends gently through woodland and scrub, and soon Florac and the valley below come into view. Head towards the west, aiming for a small ruined stone building from where a path leads downhill. Descend to a fence and then down on a path through trees.

Further down be sure to take a small path off to the left of the main track (this is just before the track divides). Emerge on the N106 at the Pont de la Bessède over the River Tarnon. Turn right if you require a campsite for the night, but to continue on the RLS Trail, cross the bridge and enter the town of Florac.

POINTS OF INTEREST

GR68

The RLS Trail follows the GR68 for about 11km westwards from the Col de la Planette. This is arguably the most scenic part of the entire journey. Much of the route follows a high ridge with extensive views of the wooded hillsides and deep-cut valleys of the Cévennes mountains. There are interesting ancient standing stones on the Col du Sapet, and the route passes through the Bois d'Altefage, the wood from where the first operation of the War of the Camisards was launched.

Tarn Valley

Those cyclists or motorists following Stevenson's route down the D998 will see the 14th-century Château de Miral on a rocky point above the river, northeast of Cocurès. The fortified collegiate church at Bédouès is also worth a visit, for those who still have the time and energy when reaching the Pont de la Pontèse.

Florac

A most attractive town situated at the foot of the high limestone cliffs of the Rocher de Rochefort, at the confluence of the rivers Tarn, Tarnon and Mimente. It lies at a point where permeable limestone meets impermeable schists, and this leads to the reappearance of a subterranean stream, the Source de Pêcher, which flows through the centre of the town down a series of terraces. Many of the medieval streets are delightful, being shaded

Water coursing through Florac

by avenues of plane trees, with many old fountains, small bridges and narrow alleyways.

Stevenson stayed the night at an inn in Rue Thérond. The 17th-century Château du Florac, mentioned by Stevenson and fortified during the War of the Camisards, is worth a visit. The main office of the Cévennes National Park, the Maison du Parc, is housed within this old castle. It is open all year and offers information on the park, displays, exhibitions and interactive presentations. Situated close to Mont Lozère, the southern Cévennes, Causse Méjean (the superb limestone plateau to the west which is ablaze with wildflowers in springtime) and the Tarn gorges, Florac is an excellent centre for a future holiday, either walking, horse/pony/cycle riding, or car touring.

Tarn Gorges

The spectacular Tarn gorges are situated further down the River Tarn, between Ispagnac (12th-century church and castle) and Sainte-Énimie, west of Florac. A visit is highly recommended, although a day would have to be set aside for this. An infrequent bus service from Florac, heading towards Mende, may be a help, but it is also worth enquiring at the tourist office, as tourist bus tours sometimes operate during the main season. Alternatively, it may be possible to hire a bicycle in Florac, so allowing access to the gorges that are within a day's ride. Look out in the town for 'Bicycles for hire' signs, or again ask at the *office de tourisme*.

STAGE 10 – *Florac to the Gare de Cassagnas*

17.4km (10.8 miles)
5hrs

Location	Distance (km)		Time (hr min)	
	Section	**Cum**	**Section**	**Cum**
Florac (546m)	0.0	0.0	0 00	0 00
Pont de Barre	1.4	1.4	0 20	0 20
Balazuègnes	7.3	8.7	2 35	2 55
Saint-Julien-d'Arpaon	1.0	9.7	0 20	3 15
Gare de Cassagnas (693m)	7.7	17.4	1 45	5 00

A short stage is called for today, after the excesses of the last two in the mountains, and a late start allows time to explore the narrow streets and alleyways of Florac before continuing on the way south. The walk is definitely 'one of two halves', as fairly strenuous hills and balcony paths above the Mimente valley contrast nicely with the easy walking along the disused railway line from Saint-Julien-d'Arpaon to the old railway station of Cassagnas. There is gorgeous countryside throughout.

FACILITIES

It is important to stock up on food for lunches and snacks in Florac before leaving, because the next shop to be encountered en route will be in Saint-Germain-de-Calberte, at the end of tomorrow's stage (although there is a possibility of buying some food at the Gare de Cassagnas).

The tiny village/hamlet of Saint-Julien-d'Arpaon, just after the half-way stage, has a *chambre d'hôte* as well as a campsite. (The future of the latter may be in some doubt, and even if it still operates, it tends to close in early September).

The remains of the old Cassagnas railway station

The day finishes at the old railway station of Cassagnas, which is about 1.5km west of the village of the same name (this old and typical Cévenol village has no facilities for tourists). The old railway station has been developed into the Espace Stevenson, a considerably extended and grotesque renovation of a once charming old building. Nevertheless, it provides much needed accommodation for RLS Trail walkers. The *chambre d'hôte* offers demi-pension and a restaurant/café. The campsite, which in 1988 was a very primitive affair with only a water tap, now has showers and a washroom and is quite a pleasant site. Meals can be purchased in the restaurant by campers as well as those staying in a *chambre d'hôte*.

TRAVELS WITH A DONKEY

The rigours of their long trek were taking effect as Stevenson and Modestine left Florac late in the afternoon of the first day of October, 'a tired donkey and tired donkey-driver'. RLS had once again spent the morning catching up on his journal and resting. The pair did not get far that day, but soon made camp in the Mimente valley, on what was to prove their last night together out in the open. Stevenson was impressed with the rocky grandeur of the valley, but the steepness of the terrain posed problems for a suitable campsite. He eventually found a spot close to the river and mused on the beauty of the starlit sky: 'No one knows the stars who has not slept, as the French happily put it, *à la belle étoile*…ignorant…of their serene and gladsome influence on the mind.'

Stevenson was awoken the next morning by the barking of a dog from a nearby house, and was soon on his way up the valley. He met only one other traveller, 'a dark and military-looking wayfarer', that morning on his walk to Cassagnas. 'I was now drawing near to Cassagnas, a cluster of black roofs upon the hillside, in this wild valley, among chestnut gardens, and looked upon in the clear air by many rocky peaks.'

It is noticeable that as he became more fatigued in the later stages of his journey, RLS made fewer entries into his journal at the time. Considerable sections were added later, when he was preparing the manuscript for *Travels with a Donkey*. However, even in the latter, relatively little is written on the final few days from Florac to Saint-Jean-du-Gard.

ROUTE

Leave **Florac** on the D907 heading south. At a roundabout follow the sign for the Camping Municipal *la tière* (two star). The GR70 is coincident with the GR43 (La Grande Draille de Margeride) for a short distance from here. There is a good footpath to the left of the road.

Ignore the first road bridge over the Tarnon (unless you want the campsite, which is on the opposite bank of the river at this point). About 700 metres after the roundabout, turn left to cross the river by the old single-span arch of the picturesque Pont de Barre. The GR43 leaves the GR70 at this point by taking the right turn after the bridge. The RLS Trail turns left uphill here on a stony path

Stage 10
Florac to the Gare de Cassagnas

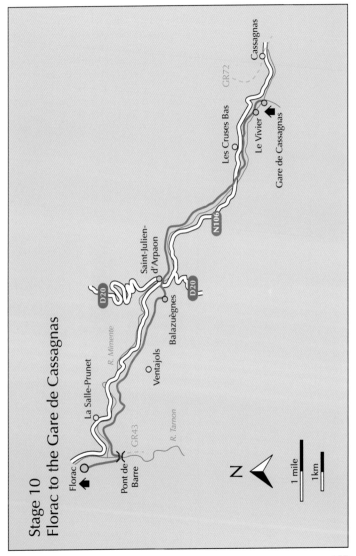

Spectacular rock face near Château de Montvaillant

signposted to Saint-Julien-d'Arpaon. You are now beginning a climb up the **Mimente valley**. ⓘ

Soon the trail descends to a surfaced track where you turn right (east), with the River Mimente now down on your left. At a T-junction turn left to cross a small bridge. Dramatic rock scenery will be seen over to the left and the impressive **Château de Montvaillant** ⓘ will come into view across the valley. A few hundred metres later at a Y-junction bear right uphill. Follow orange (horse trail markings) as well as red-and-white waymarks, ignoring a descending track off to the left. You are soon climbing high above the River Mimente, and the roofs of the village of **La Salle-Prunet** appear below left through the trees.

After over a kilometre leave this lane, which in 1.7km climbs up to the hamlet of La Borie (*gîte d'étape* and *chambres d'hôte*), by taking a wide dirt track on the left (orange and red-and-white waymarks). In just under a kilometre, about 150 metres before the track, now sur-faced, joins the N106, seen below, take a stony track climbing to the right. Soon ignore a track on the left, and for 20 metres further remain on the main track as it swings sharply to the right.

Later, ignore a track off to the right, but continue ahead (yellow paint stripe waymark). Climb now on a footpath with a narrow wooded ravine down to the left. Cross the stream, the Ruisseau des Houles, above a small waterfall, and then bear left with the stream and ravine still on your left. Climb to meet a road.

Right along this road leads to the mountain village of **Ventajols**, but the RLS Trail turns left, downhill, for about 400m. Bear right, just before a hairpin bend, onto a path through the trees, soon passing a small ruined stone building on your left. ▶

This trail, an ancient, well-made route, much overgrown in 1988, is now clear and easy to follow as it passes beneath thousands of chestnut trees, whose fruit will be strewn across the path if you are coming this way during the autumn.

The route eventually emerges from the trees to become a balcony path that swings southwards to join a track at the first houses of the village of **Balazuègnes**. Follow this track for a few hundred metres before leaving it on the left on an old cobbled footpath, descending in less than a hundred metres to a metalled lane. Turn left on this minor road to walk downhill, now re-descending into the Mimente valley. ▶

After about 600m descending on this lane, be sure to turn sharply to the right onto a footpath that descends eastwards. At the bottom turn right on the N106 for 100 metres, and then left across the bridge over the Mimente into Saint-Julien-d'Arpaon. Turn right on the far side of the bridge. Walk past the old railway station house to fol-low the old railway track to the left of the river. There now follow several kilometres of level, easy walking along the disused **Mimente railway**, ⓘ a considerable contrast to the reasonably tough walking of the morning between Florac and Saint-Julien-d'Arpaon. The walking may be easy, but the scenery in this dramatic valley is of the highest order.

The buildings and old castle of **Saint-Julien-d'Arpaon,** ⓘ men-tioned by RLS and our next destination, are seen in the valley below, over to the right.

Pass under two railway tunnels (the second bends to the left and is somewhat dark, but no torch is necessary) and over two bridges, eventually reaching the main

Looking down on Saint-Julien-d'Arpaon

N106 at Maillautier. Bear left on this road for 20 metres to rejoin the route of the old railway, now with the valley road to your left and the River Mimente to the right. Remain on the railway track, which passes through a deep cutting, and then into a third tunnel. It is advisable to keep away from the left-hand side inside this tunnel, as there may be deep holes there, but again a torch should not be necessary. The best advice is to keep to the centre of the tunnel, away from the walls.

Eventually a poorly surfaced track will be reached where you continue ahead, still with the river down to your right. Pass the few scattered buildings of Le Vivier (note the unusual 'fish' weather vane on the chimney of one of these houses) before passing through a campsite and reaching the **Gare de Cassagnas**, where accommodation will be found for the night.

POINTS OF INTEREST

Mimente Valley

The steep-sided Mimente valley is most impressive. Stevenson noted in his journal: '…steep rocky red mountains plunged down upon the narrow channel of the Mimente, their edges eaten by the rains and winds into a fantastic and precarious lacework…'

Château de Montvaillant

This is located on the opposite (north) bank of the River Mimente, 800 metres to the east of Florac.

Château de Montvaillant

Saint-Julien-d'Arpaon

The castle ruins at Saint-Julien-d'Arpaon are referred to by Stevenson as '…one [hamlet] with an old castle atop to please the heart of the tourist'. In 1617 the owner, one Jacques de Gabriac, was executed for the robbery of royal salt-tax collectors and the castle was destroyed. It was later reconstructed, but only the southern and eastern walls remain today, forming a picturesque ruin.

The Mimente Railway

The second disused railway on the RLS Trail can be followed with benefit for part of the way between Florac and Cassagnas. The history of the line is of interest. When the French railway network was being designed during the heyday of European railways, a decision was made by the French authorities to provide all *sous-préfectures* (in addition to *préfectures*) with a railway station and connecting railway. However, Florac (*sous-préfecture* of the Lozère *département*) posed a problem, as the mountainous terrain made it impractical to route the Paris–Clermont-Ferrand–Nîmes line via Florac.

The government of the day therefore granted financial assistance to the local railways *(chemin de fer départemental)* so that a single metre-wide track could be built from Florac to Sainte-Cécile-d'Andorge to join up with the main line. This was built during the late 1880s (i.e. after Stevenson's visit) using predominantly local labour to dynamite a passage for the line, construct

Easy walking on the old railway line east of Saint-Julien-d'Arpaon

the several tunnels required and lay the sleepers. The line carried both passengers and freight (mainly wood, certain minerals and lead from the Col de Jalcreste).

Pausing for breath along the old rail route

However, the parallel road in the Mimente valley had already been constructed (many new roads were being built at the time of Stevenson's visit), and with the advent of motorised transport, the line, which was a slow one, proved unpopular, although it must have been one of the most scenic railway lines in all Europe. It was eventually closed in 1948. Some of the railway sleepers were clearly visible in the late 1980s, with some alarming holes in some of the bridges, but the disused line has now been made safe and converted into a much-used walking trail.

Cassagnas

This typical old *Cévenol* village, situated about 1.5km east of the Gare de Cassagnas, now has a permanent population of little more than 20 people, and no facilities for tourists.

STAGE 11 – *Gare de Cassagnas to Saint-Germain-de-Calberte*

13.6km (8.5 miles)
4hrs 45mins

Location	Distance (km)		Time (hr min)	
	Section	Cum	Section	Cum
Gare de Cassagnas (693m)	0.0	0.0	0 00	0 00
Col de la Pierre Plantée (891m)	9.8	9.8	3 30	3 30
Saint-Germain-de-Calberte (480m)	3.8	13.6	1 15	4 45

Another short stage today, in most attractive country. Beginning with a pleasant and easy climb up through woodland, heading generally southwards towards the Plan de Fontmort, then a determined turn to the east to follow tracks and the GR7 and GR67, and later the GR67A, to reach the Col de la Pierre Plantée (891m), where an ancient standing stone will be found. Next it is downhill all the way through woodland until a final turning brings you into Saint-Germain-de-Calberte.

FACILITIES
No chance of refreshments today on a route that passes no places of habitation until Le Serre de la Can, a little before Saint-Germain-de-Calberte. The latter has a good *épicerie*, a *boulangerie*, post office, tourist office, restaurant, bar/café, and another café that is part of the village *gîte d'étape*. There are *chambres d'hôte* in the centre of the village and a *relais d'étape* (hotel/bar/restaurant) at Le Serre de la Can in the woods about a kilometre to the northwest of Saint-Germain-de-Calberte, passed en route. The campsite is 1.3km from the village and downhill, and as such cannot be particularly recommended for the RLS Trail walker.

As the stage is only a short one, some walkers may prefer to advance a few more kilometres along the trail, maybe to the Pont de Burgen where there is a *gîte d'étape*, or further to Saint-Étienne-Vallée-Française which has *chambres d'hôte* accommodation (see Stage 12).

TRAVELS WITH A DONKEY

Stevenson had lunch at the inn at Cassagnas in the company of 'a gendarme and a merchant', the latter considering Stevenson's journey to be foolhardy and dangerous. RLS approved of the villagers, who 'seemed intelligent after a countrified fashion, and were all plain and dignified in manner'.

'A little after two' Stevenson left Cassagnas and 'struck across the Mimente and took a rugged path southward up a hillside covered with loose stones and turfs of heather', marvelling at 'perhaps the wildest view of all my journey'. He traversed the Col des Laupies and was directed to the road for Saint-Germain-de-Calberte by a very old shepherd, who mistook Stevenson for a pedlar. On the descent he was overtaken by nightfall but assisted by a bright moon, 'purified nocturnal sunshine', until this went behind a hill and he pursued his way 'in great darkness'. He entered Saint-Germain-de-Calberte, which was 'asleep and silent, and buried in opaque night' and stayed the night at the village inn.

Brutal modernisation of the old Cassagnas railway station

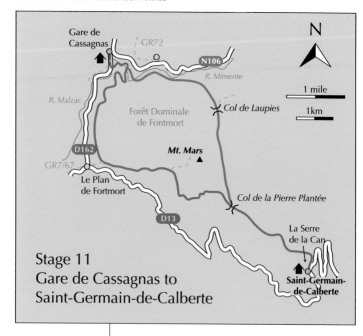

Stage 11
Gare de Cassagnas to
Saint-Germain-de-Calberte

ROUTE

Twenty metres after the *gare* you should find a GR72
sign indicating the way to the Barre des Cévennes. Bear
right here to cross an iron bridge (Le Pont du Croupatas)
over the River Mimente. Bear left, now with the river on
your left, but in a few hundred metres turn left to cross a
bridge. Keep to the main track as it climbs first to the
north, then south, then north and finally south again.

Later ignore a track on the left and continue ahead
(west). In a further 400 metres ignore a track descending
to the right. The pleasant woodland path climbs gently
for over 2km until it reaches a small clearing at a cross-
tracks. Descend ahead to meet a track T-junction to the
east of the **Plan de Fontmort**. ⓘ Turn left (east) on a
descending track signposted to the Reservoir de
Fontmort (GR70, GR67 and GR7). ◀

To see the monument
to the Camisards'
revolt, turn to the
right at the track T-
junction to walk to
the Plan de Fontmort,
about 400 metres to
the southwest.

This track is the old road to Saint-Germain-de-Calberte and presents fine views of the distant 'blue' mountains. Soon pass the Reservoir de Fontmort on your left, and later ignore a grassy track descending to the right, but remain on the main track ahead on the wooded ridge. At the next Y-junction keep left uphill, still on the main track.

About 2km after the Reservoir de Fontmort you will reach a major Y-junction where the GR routes divide. The GR7 and GR67 (E4) go to the left (towards the Col de Jalcreste), but the RLS Trail takes the right fork, the GR70, which in this area is coincident with the GR67A, signposted to Le Serre de la Can in 6km. After about 1.5km ignore a signposted path sharply off to the right to Saint Clemént (0.5km) and Malafosse (2km). Continue on the clearly defined track, along which the scent of pine trees is intoxicating, to reach the Col de la Pierre Plantée, on which sits a large upright waymarker stone. ▶

Ancient waymarker stone at the Col de la Pierre Plantée

The summit and viewpoint of Mont Mars (1162m/5809ft), the highest point in the area, is to the northwest of the **Col de la Pierre Plantée,** and can be reached by a detour of about 1.5km (see IGN map).

167

There is a junction of four paths at the col. Take the second left of these, signposted to **Le Serre de la Can** in 2.5km on the GR70 and GR67A. After about 100 metres ignore a track off to the left, but continue ahead on the main track, which gradually descends. The trail becomes a wide unsurfaced forest road that descends to a reservoir on the right at a hairpin bend. Fifty metres after this bend turn sharply to the right off the main forest road onto a track. This track descends through the trees to reach a large signpost for Saint-Germain-de-Calberte on the right and a sign for a *relais d'étape* (hotel/bar/restaurant, Le Petit Calbertois) on the left.

Descend ahead over rock slabs to reach a wide **forest ⓘ track**. Turn left here to descend around a hairpin bend. Descend to where the wide track comes to an abrupt end and here follow a narrow footpath down through trees. The waymarked trail zigzags down through the wood to meet a track. Turn right downhill on this, continuing to zigzag down to join the road at **Saint-Germain-de-Calberte** ⓘ ('…I was shot without preparation into Saint-Germain-de-Calberte…'). Turn right to walk downhill through the village to the church at its centre.

Alternative Route from the Gare de Cassagnas to the Col de la Pierre Plantée via the Col des Laupies

An alternative route to the Col de la Pierre Plantée can be taken, which more closely follows the route taken by Stevenson, but it involves a long section of walking on an unwaymarked forest road. For this route follow the GR72 from the Gare de Cassagnas, continuing eastwards along the old disused railway line along the Mimente valley before leaving it to climb on an old drove road to the **Col des Laupies** (1001m). From here continue south on a forest road to reach the Col de la Pierre Plantée, where the route described above is re-joined.

POINTS OF INTEREST

Plan de Fontmort (Font Morte)
Here is a monument, erected in 1887 (i.e. after Stevenson's visit), to the Camisards' revolt. According to RLS, this is the place where 'Poul with his Armenian sabre slashed down the Camisards of Séguier'.

The hillsides hereabouts are dotted with numerous caves used as hideaways by the Camisards in the 18th century, and later by resistance fighters during the Second World War.

Menhirs
There are several ancient standing stones along the route, in particular at the Plan de Fontmort, the Col de la Pierre Plantée (as the name suggests) and, on the alternative route, at the Col des Laupies.

Watershed
The hills between the Mimente valley and Saint-Germain-de-Calberte form an important watershed. Behind, all the streams and rivers flow eventually into the Garonne and so on to the Atlantic (or 'western ocean'). Ahead, the waters drain into the Rhône and thence to the Mediterranean.

Forestry
The whole area is heavily forested. This is in sharp contrast to Stevenson's day, when centuries of transhumance (the movement of tens of thousands of animals from lowland to upland pasture in spring, and back again in the autumn) had stripped the land of vegetation and topsoil. A policy to plant trees and so combat the erosion was implemented by a government official, Georges Fabre, in 1875. As can now be witnessed, this afforestation programme was highly successful. (Beware of possible future changes to the line of the RLS Trail as a result of forestry operations – any diversions should hopefully be well signposted.)

Chestnuts

Chestnut trees, much admired by RLS, are common on the hillsides of the Cévennes, and appear in their hundreds of thousands along the RLS Trail, particularly south of Florac They are a joy to see, particularly when walking the trail in late September, when the chestnuts are ripe. In the 16th century, the chestnut was the staple diet of the population, and even in Stevenson's day was an important source of food and income. Chestnuts were eaten fresh, in soups or stews, or were dried and ground into flour for bread (the 'tree of bread'). No part of the tree was wasted: the wood was used to build furniture, the inner bark for basket making and the foliage was fed to livestock. This is in stark contrast to the situation today, where millions of the chestnuts are left to rot on the ground.

Chestnuts

Saint-Germain-de-Calberte

A pleasant southern mountain town which remained Catholic during the War of the Camisards. There are plane trees in the small square and flowers decorate the many terraced gardens. The 12th-century Romanesque church has an interesting decorated doorway. The Abbè du Chayla, whose murder started the War of the Camisards (see Le Pont-de-Montvert, Stage 8), is buried inside the church.

21.4km (13.3 miles)
7hrs 15mins

Location	Distance (km)		Time (hr. min)	
	Section	**Cum**	**Section**	**Cum**
Saint-Germain-de-Calberte (480m)	0.0	0.0	0 00	0 00
Saint-Étienne-Vallée-Française	8.9	8.9	2 50	2 50
Le Martinet	1.2	10.1	0 25	3 15
Col de Saint-Pierre (597m)	3.3	13.4	1 30	4 45
Signal de Saint-Pierre (695m)	0.3	13.7	0 20	5 05
Col de Saint-Pierre (597m)	0.3	14.0	0 15	5 20
Pied-de-Côte	3.4	17.4	0 55	6 15
Saint-Jean-du-Gard (190m)	4.0	21.4	1 00	7 15

The day begins with a pleasant stroll on an ancient path through chestnut groves to descend to the valley which leads to the village of Saint-Étienne-Vallée-Française. A long climb up to Col de Saint-Pierre follows, from where a short detour to the summit of Saint-Pierre is a highlight of the day. The 360 degree view from the top will allow you to say a fond farewell to the Cévennes mountains, which you have now nearly completely traversed. A steep path descends from the col down to the attractive hamlet of Pied-de-Côte, and from there a final walk alongside the River Gardon leads into Saint-Jean-du-Gard, the destination you have sought for so long.

FACILITIES

In Saint-Étienne-Vallée-Française you will find two *épiceries* and a *boulangerie*, as well as a café/restaurant, passed en route. There is a bank here also, but it is seldom open. Several accommodation choices are available – the *gîte d'étape* at the Pont de Burgen between Saint-Germain-de-Calberte and Saint-Étienne-Vallée-Française, a *chambres d'hôte* passed en route between

Gushing waters of the River Gardon

Saint-Étienne-Vallée-Française and Le Martinet, and a hotel next to the bridge over the River Gardon de Sainte-Croix at Le Martinet – before the climb up to Col Saint-Pierre.

Campers have the choice of several campsites passed or signposted from the route, one about 2km before Saint-Jean-du-Gard being particularly well placed (the nearest campsite to Saint-Jean is probably Les Sources, north-northeast of the town on the D50, about a kilometre from the centre).

Saint-Jean-du-Gard has several hotels, the first of which is passed en route a little way after the D907/D260A road junction (Le Raset suburb on the town's outskirts). Although the inn that RLS stayed in has long gone, a modern hotel/restaurant named after Stevenson is one of the hotels in the centre. Shops, restaurants and cafés abound in Saint-Jean, which also has banks and tourist and post offices. Gift shops will be found in the town if presents or souvenirs are sought at the end of the holiday, but better selections are available in Alès and at Nîmes. Those wishing to leave Saint-Jean by public transport will find the bus station on the main street, a little past the *mairie*.

TRAVELS WITH A DONKEY

RLS stayed the morning in Saint-Germain-de-Calberte, a 'little Catholic metropolis, a thimblefull of Rome, in such a wild and contrary neighbourhood', claiming that he had '…not often enjoyed a place more deeply'. However, his thoughts were elsewhere: 'Perhaps someone was thinking of me in another country.' He was missing Fanny Osbourne terribly, and longed to reach Alès where he hoped for news from her.

Stevenson dined and took coffee with two Catholics, and as a result did not leave Saint-Germain-de-Calberte until '…long past three', nevertheless, he was determined to reach Saint-Jean-du-Gard without an intermediary stop. He and Modestine passed through Saint-Étienne-Vallée-Française, 'or Val Francesque as they used to call it; and towards evening began to ascend the hill of St. Pierre'. Modestine was goaded without mercy on this 'long and steep ascent' because Stevenson 'dearly desired to see the view upon the other side before the day had faded'. However, it was dark by the time they reached the summit (presumably the col) where they ate their last meal together. The outline of Mont Aigoual was clearly visible in the moonlight as the pair made the 'long descent upon St Jean du Gard'. They arrived in the town very late at night: 'Before ten o'clock we had got in and were at supper; fifteen miles and a stiff hill in little beyond six hours.'

Stevenson had originally intended to continue on foot to Alès. Soon after leaving Le Monastier, and having problems persuading Modestine to follow the trail, he had declared that: 'The thought that this was to last from here to Alais nearly broke my heart.' However, he was impatient to reach Alès for his letters, and when Modestine was declared unfit for travel on the following day, he decided to sell the donkey and take the stagecoach.

Restored old mas (farmhouse) seen from the RLS Trail in the southern Cévennes

Modestine was sold, 'saddle and all', for 35 francs, considerably less than he had paid for her. She lived in happy retirement for several years with the man who bought her, and is buried in a field in Saint-Jean. The innkeeper back in Cheylard-l'Évêque had told RLS that before a few days he '...should care to love Modestine like a dog', and so it seemed, as he wept for the animal on his journey to Alès. 'For twelve days we had been fast companions; we had travelled upwards of a hundred and twenty miles, crossed several respectable ridges and jogged along with our six legs by many a rocky and many a boggy by-road.'

ROUTE

Walk through **Saint-Germain-de-Calberte** on the D984, bearing right to pass the *épicerie*. About 300 metres after leaving the village on the D984, take a marked surfaced track off to the right, signposted to **Les Faïsses** and Les Moles. After 200 metres ignore a path off to the left to a building, but continue to climb on the track ahead, later ignoring another track that turns sharply to the right. Keep to the main track to meet and cross a road, the D13.

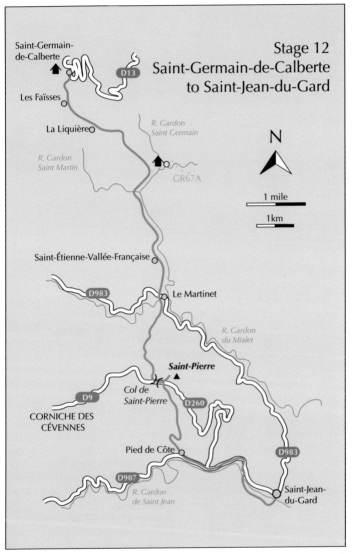

Old coppiced trees alongside the ancient route that leaves at Saint-Germain-de-Calberte

Descend passing several houses, with good views to the left. Holm oaks and chestnut trees hang over the trail. Go ahead at a cross-tracks and descend by a series of zigzags, remaining on the main track, ignoring side turnings. Eventually the trail swings to the left by a large and old rubbish tip (alas, this has been here since at least 1988, when I was first here!). About 300 metres after the tip ignore a track on the left, but remain ahead on the main track, eventually dropping to meet the D984.

Locate an unmarked grassy path almost opposite. This descends quite steeply down through trees for 100 metres to a minor road. ◀ Turn right to follow the narrow road to the D984 at a hairpin bend. Turn left, cross the bridge over the river and continue on this main road, which usually carries little traffic, with the river to the left.

Those wanting overnight accommodation at the gîte d'étape at the Pont de Burgen should turn left along the minor road for about 450 metres – this is the route of the GR67A.

After about a kilometre of road walking ignore a minor road on the right, signposted to Le Masbernat. About 150 metres later bear right on an earthen track

176

signposted to Dourmen. Pass this house and keep ahead on the track, which climbs above and runs parallel with the road. At the high point of this road the roofs of the village of Saint-Étienne-Vallée-Française come into view ahead. The track becomes surfaced and drops to the main road a little before the village. Turn right along the road to head south, so entering **Saint-Étienne-Vallée-Française**, ⓘ where ample refreshments may be had before continuing on the last stage of the RLS Trail to Saint-Jean-du-Gard.

New road and old bridge at the entrance to Saint-Étienne-Vallée-Française

Exit the village on the D984. A hundred metres after the road sign indicating the limit of Saint-Étienne-Vallée-Française, turn right onto an earthen track. At a track junction a further 100 metres along, turn sharply to the left uphill. Climb steeply to pass Lancize *chambre d'hôte*. At the top of the climb descend on a footpath.

Take the less steep path to the left when you arrive at a track junction (the very steep one on the right soon meets up with the path that you have taken) to descend

*Looking down to
Le Martinet*

to the road junction of the D984 with the D983. Take the latter road, signposted to Saint-Jean-du-Gard, and in 250 metres pass **Le Martinet** bar/restaurant, then cross the bridge over the River Gardon de Sainte Croix. On the far side of the bridge turn right on the path signposted to Col de Saint-Pierre.

The trail climbs in zigzags at first, before maintaining a magnetic bearing of 208 degrees (south-south-west). After a final steep section on this stony path, you will reach a track where you turn right, continuing to climb steadily. This eventually emerges on the D9 (the **Corniche des Cévennes** ①), at which point the climb is virtually over. Turn left, ascending gently to reach the **Col de Saint-Pierre** (597m).

The RLS Trail descends to the Pied-de-Côte from the col, but if time and energy are plentiful, and the weather settled, then an excursion from here to the summit of **Saint-Pierre**, ① from which there are tremendous, extensive views of the Cévennes, is strongly recommended – although not for those who are unsure of their ability to navigate on a steep mountainside. Particular care has to be taken with navigation while on this detour, as the consequences of becoming lost on this mountainside could be severe. ▸

No one should attempt it during heavy rain or when a thick mist covers the hillside.

Start the climb to the summit at the signpost on the col indicating 'Table d'Orientation du Signal de Saint-Pierre, durée 20 minutes (Sentier Escarpé)'. The thin path through the trees is waymarked with yellow paint stripes, heading generally east-northeast to reach the viewpoint and orientation table on the summit (695m). Take special care not to lose the waymarks while on this ascent. It is advisable to return to the col by the reverse of the route of ascent.

There is also another route to the top, which takes a path that first traverses the northern side of the mountain, emerging at a wide path heading southeast uphill to the orientation table on the western summit. The view from here is outstanding, with many of the principal hills of the Cévennes on display. These can be identified by means of the *table d'orientation* (viewpoint indicator). The route that you have taken from Saint-Germain-de-Calberte can easily be traced.

There are two tops on the summit area – on one stands the *table d'orientation*, and the other is some 40 metres to the east. The remains of an IGN triangulation survey point – a short metal stump in the rock – is located on the latter. Blue-and-white waymarks lead from the *table d'orientation* to this eastern summit, and they continue on a scrambly descent eastwards. A descent of the mountain by this route should only be attempted by the adventurous and experienced.

Return to the Col de Saint-Pierre, where you will find a picnic area and stone shelter, as well as an old marker post for the Route Royale No 107. ▸ The col also marks the boundary between the Lozère and Gard *départements*.

The modern road over the Col de Saint-Pierre was once part of this ancient route, which ran from Nîmes to Saint-Flour.

A traverse of the Lozère is now almost complete. A few metres before the road sign indicating the Département du Gard, take a steep rocky path on the

RLS Trail walker on the descent to Pied-de-Côte

right waymarked with red-and-white (GR70) and yellow (PR11) paint flashes and signposted to Saint-Jean-du-Gard in 7km. So begin a long descent of almost 400m loss in altitude to Pied-de-Côte, on an excellent, narrow rocky footpath, possibly the best of the whole RLS Trail.

The trail descends to pass a building on the right and a house on the left (L'Affenadou) where you continue ahead now on a descending track. Follow this drove road, which soon becomes surfaced as it descends to the northwest and later to the southeast to reach the D907 at **Pied-de-Côte** (220m), a charming small and ancient hamlet.

Turn left to follow the D907 in the direction of **Saint-Jean-du-Gard**, above and alongside the River Gardon on your right (take special care of passing traffic on this main road). A campsite is passed on your right a little before the junction with the D260. Continue ahead on the D907 until about 400 metres after the junction with

Old bridge over the River Gardon

the D260A (signposted to Cachar), and a few metres before a hotel on the left, turn right on a minor road that crosses the Gardon river.

Turn left on the far side of the bridge to follow a surfaced track to reach a house. Here the trail becomes a sandy track that soon narrows into a path that follows the River Gardon now on your left. Pass under the arch of the first road bridge over the Gardon, turn right for 50 metres, then left to follow a lane alongside houses to arrive at Saint-Jean-du-Gard railway station on your right. Turn left at this point to walk over the bridge into town.

Before reaching the *mairie* look out for the RLS memorial on the left-hand side of the road, commemorating the end of Stevenson's walk at Saint-Jean-du-Gard. Note that, sadly, the date given on this memorial for RLS's arrival in the town is 2 October 1878, when it was in fact the third of that month.

.ommemo-
ɪnson's arrival
ıt-Jean-du-Gard

POINTS OF INTEREST

Saint-Étienne-Vallée-Française
The château overlooking the river and the ancient bridge are the main items of interest. There is an old beacon tower between Saint-Étienne-Vallée-Française and Le Martinet.

Corniche des Cévennes
The name given to the high mountain road linking Barre-des-Cévennes to Saint-Jean-du-Gard. Built as a military road during the reign of Louis XIV, it is a considerable feat of engineering.

Saint-Pierre (695m)
There is a superb viewpoint from the *table d'orientation* on the summit. The wooded hillsides of the Cévennes stretch, seemingly endlessly, to the north, while the valley of the Gardon, journey's end, lies far below. A time for reflection.

EPILOGUE
Part 1 – Saint-Jean-du-Gard and Mas Soubeyran, Alès and Nîmes: 'The Last Day'

Stevenson did not stay long in Saint-Jean-du-Gard ('I was now eager to reach Alais [Alès] for my letters…'), but those who have followed his journey south from Le Monastier are advised, if time is available, to relax after the labours of their walk and explore the town before returning home or continuing further on foot to Mialet or Alès (see Epilogue, Part 2).

Saint-Jean-du-Gard is a pleasant southern town whose motto in the old Occitan language is, 'Al Sourel de la Liberta' ('In the Sunlight of Freedom'). The attractions of the town include the following.

1   The ancient town **ramparts**, **clock tower** and old **bridge** across the River Gardon.
2   **Musée des Vallées Cévenoles** (Cévenol Valleys Museum). Housed in a 17th-century *auberge*, the museum covers all aspects of Cévenol life, including chestnut culture and the old silk industry. Audio guide in English. Open every day from April to October and three days a week from November to March.
3   **Train à Vapeur des Cévennes** (the steam railway). From the beginning of April to the end of October steam trains run daily from the station in Saint-Jean-du-Gard (south of the river) to Anduze. Some of the locomotives are British made. It is possible to take a bus from Anduze to Alès, so this pleasant tourist train could be used as part of your journey home.

Provided the walker has not, unlike Modestine, been 'pronounced unfit for travel', there are a number of local walks that explore the country around Saint-Jean-du-Gard. These are clearly waymarked with blue-and-white and blue paint stripes and are from one to several hours

183

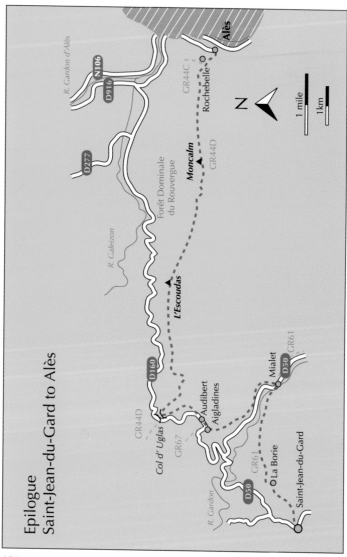

Epilogue
Saint-Jean-du-Gard to Alès

in duration. Details from the tourist office. Those looking for something more ambitious are recommended to take the circular Tour des Cévennes – the 130km (81 mile) GR67. This can be joined at Mialet to the east, or at the Col de Ascliér to the west, by following the GR61 from Saint-Jean-du-Gard (see Appendix 2). A French Topo guide to the walk can be purchased locally.

Mas Soubeyran

The highly recommended Musée du Désert at Mas Soubeyran (www.museedudesert.com) is particularly relevant for RLS Trail walkers who have recently traversed the country (Le Pays Camisard) in which the terrible events of the War of the Camisards were played out. The museum is just beyond Mialet on the D50 (bus, 15 minutes from Saint-Jean-du-Gard, or walk there – see Epilogue, Part 2).

The museum is contained in the house, situated amongst rather austere mountain scenery, where the Camisard leader Rolland was born. The exhibition, spread over 15 rooms, depicts the traditional lifestyle of the Cévenol people and outlines the Protestant struggle of the 18th century, some of which is so vividly described by Stevenson. The names of many of those who lost their lives in the War of the Camisards are written on the walls in gold lettering. Audio-visual presentation. Open every day from 1 March to 30 November. Restaurant/café

Alès

The only city of any appreciable size in the area, situated in the wide, low plain to the east of the Cévennes mountains. Whatever your ultimate direction of travel after Saint-Jean-du-Gard, you will probably go first to Alés, by bus or on foot, before going home. It is a large commercial and industrial town of little interest to the tourist, but there is a good shopping centre where presents or souvenirs of the region can be bought.

Alés was once at the heart of a productive mining area in France, and the city now has a mining museum and a 'show mine' which is open to visitors. The latter is in the suburb of Alés-Rochebelle and is passed en route in the latter stages of the walk to Alés (described in Part 2, below). There are several large hotels in the city, and a *chambre d'hôte*, the Mas de Rochebelle, which provides especially for walkers and is passed on the walk into Alés from Mialet (see Part 2, below).

If time is available, a trip to Nîmes can be recommended. The city can be reached from Saint-Jean-du-Gard either directly by bus, or by bus first to Alés and then by main-line train. Nîmes is rich in antiquities, with the magnificent Roman amphitheatre in the centre of the city, the most complete to survive from the Roman Empire, being the main attraction. Other places of interest include the Maison Carrée (Roman temple and museum, with audio-visual theatre), Temple of Diana, Roman bathhouse and ornamental gardens (Quai de la Fontaine), Porte d'Auguste (Roman gateway), Tour Magne (watchtower) and the Museum of Old Nîmes. There is a youth hostel (although it is a bus ride out of the city centre), as well as many hotels of all categories.

Part 2 – Walking to Mialet or to Alès

Stevenson took a stagecoach to Alés, but those with the time and inclination can reach it on foot by making use of the several interconnecting waymarked long-distance GR trails in the region. The route is via Mialet and the Col d'Uglas, before heading east on a long wooded ridge that finally peters out on the very edge of the outskirts of Alés.

A word of caution is required, however. The distance between Saint-Jean-du-Gard and Alés is no more than some of the longer stages of the RLS Trail, but the time required to walk it will be greater, as the terrain from the Col d'Uglas to Alés is far more difficult to negotiate than any of the previous stages from Le Puy. In addition, there is no opportunity to acquire water or other refreshments between Mialet and Alés, so this stage should only be attempted by fit, experienced, well-prepared and well-equipped walkers.

Nevertheless, the initial walk from Saint-Jean-du-Gard to Mialet is easy and a delight, and once at Mialet the excellent Musée du Désert at Mas Soubeyran can be visited (see Epilogue, Part 1). This stage to Mialet will probably satisfy most people who want to explore a little more after Saint-Jean-du-Gard.

Part 2 – Saint-Jean-du-Gard to Mialet

6km (3.7 miles)
1hr 50mins

Location	Distance (km)		Time (hr min)	
	Section	Cum	Section	Cum
Saint-Jean-du-Gard (190m)	0.0	0.0	0 00	0 00
Mialet (161m)	6.0	6.0	1 50	1 50

The route is a section of the GR61. There are *chambres d'hôte* at Mialet and a restaurant/café in the Musée du Désert at Mas Soubeyran.

ROUTE

Leave **Saint-Jean-du-Gard** heading northeast, passing the *mairie* (note interesting murals) on your right and then the bus station (for buses to Mialet and Alès) also on your right. Walk along the road signposted to Mialet on Avenue Abraham Mazel, soon turning right following a signpost for the GR61 to the Quartier de Luc and the Gymnase des Fumades. Later, be sure to take the left, lower fork at a Y-junction (GR61 waymark).

Leave the road at a hairpin bend to the right, by bearing left onto a narrow surfaced lane. Follow a sign to Bajanas and Montezorgues. On reaching a Y-junction take the right fork signposted to Montezorgues (not the left one signposted to Mialet). A hundred metres later

View of the Pont des Camisards at Mialet

leave the surfaced lane on a stony track on the left. This is another ancient balcony path, which offers fine views over the wooded hilly country to the north. The Mialet river is below to your left and the path, expertly engineered on a rocky shelf, gradually descends to meet a surfaced track which itself descends to the river to cross the ancient Pont des Camisards, a very picturesque spot. Here is the junction of the GR61 and GR67. Turn right to visit the village of **Mialet**, or left to continue the walk to Alès.

Part 2 – Mialet to Alès

20km (12.4 miles)
8hrs 15mins

Location	Distance (km)		Time (hr min)	
	Section	Cum	Section	Cum
Mialet (161m)	0.0	0.0	0 00	0 00
Aïgladines	3.1	3.1	1 00	1 00
Col d'Uglas (539m)	2.1	5.2	0 45	1 45
L'Escoudas (656m)	5.2	10.4	2 30	4 15
Col de Mayelle (469m)	2.8	13.2	1 20	5 35
Moncalm (563m)	0.8	14.0	0 25	6 00
Croix de Sauvage	1.9	15.9	0 45	6 45
Alès – Rochebelle	2.1	18.0	0 45	7 30
Alès – railway station (125m)	2.0	20.0	0 45	8 15

Note No water or other refreshments are available between Mialet and Alès.

The route uses a section of the GR67 from Mialet to Aïgladines, then a local trail to the Col d'Uglas and finally the GR44D for several kilometres eastwards along the ridge and down to Alès.

After little more than 3km of easy track walking from the Col d'Uglas, the 'grade' of the walk suddenly increases considerably until the Croix de Sauvage is reached, about 4km before the centre of Alès. Much of the route is now on narrow footpaths enclosed within a dense undergrowth of trees and bushes. Progress is slow as the ground is often rough, sometimes very steep, and there are sections over limestone pavement and on abrupt, precipitous limestone edges that are potentially hazardous, particularly in wet weather. The distance form the Col d'Uglas to the Croix de Sauvage is little more than 12km, but the 5 hours' time given indicates the severity of the terrain.

The other problem is that there is no possibility of acquiring water between Mialet and Alés, so that in hot weather – and it is often very hot indeed here during the summer months – this would be a serious consideration. As a very long section of the route follows a high ridge, it should not be attempted if thunderstorms are predicted.

Despite all these cautions, however, the walk is an excellent one, and should present no real problems for fit, suitably prepared and equipped walkers in good weather conditions.

ROUTE

Leave **Mialet** by walking north along the D50 for about 600 metres before leaving it for a surfaced lane climbing to the right towards some houses (Les Clapiers). Leave this lane where it bends sharply to the right by continuing ahead, climbing on a stony track. This is yet another old *draille* (drove road), climbing gradually to the north to reach the hamlet of **Aïgladines**, where the GR67 leaves our trail by bearing left under a stone arch. (Note that there is a GR70 waymark here, although this *grande randonnée* officially ends in Saint-Jean-du-Gard.)

Turn to the right here (yellow-and-white waymarks) on a narrow surfaced lane through the hamlet, turning right again at a T-junction, heading for a second hamlet, that of **Audibert**. Now climb on the D160 until just after a hairpin bend to the left, leaving the road to continue the ascent on a track to the right, following both yellow-and-white and red-and-white waymarking.

After a few metres, be sure to turn sharp left to climb on an excellent old path, which unfortunately is poorly waymarked (there are but one or two yellow paint marks and no red-and-white markings). The trail heads firstly to the northeast and then to the northwest. Eventually a house (Les Combes) is seen over to the left, then the D160 is soon encountered at the **Col d'Uglas** (539m).

There is a GR44D waymark at the col indicating the Croix de Sauvage in 4 hours and Alés-Rochebelle in 5 hours 30 minutes. Turn right at the col to follow the main track. After about a kilometre it is worth the short detour to the right to visit the *table d'orientation*, from where there is a superb view out over the Cévennes hills. The information board here points out many of the hills and villages that you have visited on your journey so far.

Les Combes

The track changes direction several times as it gradually climbs into the hills. About 3km after the Col d'Uglas keep ahead at a cross tracks, following red-and-white and red-and-yellow (*GR de pays*) waymarks, now following the ridge eastwards. The track soon becomes a narrow footpath through trees and scrub. Be sure to follow the red-and-white waymarks carefully, and take special care on sections of limestone pavement and near precipitous edges – remember that help is far away.

The ridge undulates with some steep ascents and descents. The first principal summit reached is an unnamed 670m top, followed by the summit of **L'Escoudas** (656m), where there is a small IGN triangulation survey point. From L'Escoudas the trail descends to the Col de L'Escoudas (615m), where there is a signpost indicating that you have come 5.5km from the Col d'Uglas on the GR44D and that it is 2.5km further to the Col de Mayelle and 4km to Moncalm.

The next couple of kilometres are fairly straightforward, before a steep and rough descent to the **Col de Mayelle** (469m). Here there is a junction of five tracks and a signpost indicating 2km ahead to the Muraille du Moncalm and 6.5km to Alés. From the Col de Mayelle follow the track climbing towards Moncalm, later leaving the track for a rocky path on the left. Follow red-and-white and yellow waymarks to reach the summit of **Moncalm** (563m), where three *tables d'orientation* will be found, one facing north, one to the southwest and one to the east, with the city of Alés outstretched far below.

After admiring the extensive all-round views from the large summit area, leave the top following yellow and red-and-white waymarks to reach a signpost at the Muraille du Moncalm (500m). The signpost here indicates that it is now 2km to the Croix de Sauvage and 4.5km to Alés by the GR44D. From here climb to spot height 506. Descend on a narrow, sometimes steep path to arrive at a wide track. Turn left here (no waymark at this point), but later follow waymarks to the Croix de Sauvage at an altitude of 300m. This is a large old metal cross, 500 metres from the ruins of the 14th-century Château de Sauvage.

From the **Croix de Sauvage** the route down to the outskirts of Alés is adequately waymarked with red-and-white stripes, the last you will encounter on this walking trip in France. The trail changes direction several times, but eventually reaches a road near a 'show mine'. You have now arrived in the **Rochebelle** district of Alés.

From here walk down to the Faubourg-de-Rochebelle and from there follow the 'Centre Ville' signs – the city centre is a little over a kilometre from here. There is a main-line railway station (e.g. for trains south to Nîmes or north to Paris) and several hotels. (You passed a *chambre d'hôte*, the Mas de Rochebelle, when the GR44D met the road on arriving in the outskirts of the city.)

APPENDIX 1

GÎTES D'ÉTAPE ON OR CLOSE TO THE RLS TRAIL

Note: When phoning France from the UK, dial 00 33 and omit the first zero shown in the phone numbers below and those in Appendix 5.

Le Puy-en-Velay
(i) Youth hostel. Centre Pierre Cardinal, Rue Jules Vallès. Near the cathedral. 55 places. Tel 04 71.05.52.40.
(ii) *Gîte d'étape* des Capucins. 29 Rue des Capucins. 19 places. Tel 04.71.04.28.74.
(iii) *Gîte d'étape* Saint-François. 19 places. Tel 04.71.05.98.86.
Le Monastier-sur-Gazeille
(i) *Gîte d'étape* Emmanul Falgon. 32 Rue Langlade. 10 places. Tel 04.71.03.84.74, e-mail gite.monastier@hotmail.fr.
(ii) *Gîte d'étape communal*. Rue Saint-Jean. 19 places. Tel 04.71.03.82.37.

Goudet
Gîte d'étape du Pipet. 19 places. Tel 04.71.57.18.05, e-mail massebeuf.rocher@wanadoo.fr.

Le Bouchet-Saint-Nicolas
The old *Gîte d'étape* communal closed in 2006 and a new *Gîte d'étape* opened in 2007. Contact the Auberge Le Couvige in the centre of the village for details, tel 04.71.57.32.32.

Pradelles
Gîte d'étape. Key from the Brasserie du Musée on the high street opposite the road down to the Place de la Halle. 12 places. Tel 04.71.00.87.88, e-mail gilles.romond@wanadoo.fr.

Cheylard-l'Évêque
Refuge du Moure. This establishment, located opposite the church in the centre of the village, is both a *Gîte d'étape* and a *chambres d'hote*. 33 places, no kitchen. Tel 04.66.69.03.21, website www.lozere-gite.com.

La Bastide-Puylaurent
Gîte d'étape L'étoile. 19 places. Tel 04.66.46.05.52, e-mail welcome@etoile.fr.

Chasseradès/Mirandol
Gîte d'étape Le Mirandol. On the route of the RLS Trail just over a kilometre after Chasseradès. 15 places. Tel 04.66.46.01.14, website www.hotel-des-sources.fr.

Les Alpiers
Gîte d'étape. 15 places. Tel 04.66.48.67.19.

Station le Mont Lozère
Gîte d'étape Le Refuge. Tel 04.66.48.62.83.
Le Pont-de-Montvert
Gîte d'étape communal. In the Ecomuseum building. 35 places. Contact the *mairie*, tel 04.66.45.80.10.

Mijavols
Gîte d'étape 3.5km off-route between Le Pont-de-Montvert and Florac in the area of the Signal du Bougès. 20 places. Tel 04.66.45.09.04.

Florac
(i) *Gîte d'étape* La Carline. 18 Rue du Pêcher. 18 places. Tel 04.66.45.24.54, website www.causses-cevennes.com/lagrave.htm, e-mail lagrave.alain@wanadoo.fr.
(ii) *Gîte d'étape* communal. 29 places. Tel 04.66.45.14.93.

Gare de Cassagnes
Espace Stevenson. *Chambres d'hôte* and camping. 25 places. Tel 04.66.45.20.34.

Saint-Germain-de-Calberte
Gîte d'étape Le Recantou. In the centre of the village by the post office. 10 places. Tel 04.66.45.90.34.

Pont de Burgen
Gîte d'étape about 500 metres off-route between Saint-Germain-de-Calberte and Saint-Étienne-Vallée-Française. 21 places. Tel 04.66.45.75.30 or 04.66.45.73.94, website www.gite-randos-cevennes.com, e-mail gites-randos.cevennes@wanadoo.fr.

There are several other *gîtes d'étape* in the Velay, Gévaudan, Vivarais and Cévennes, but all some distance from the RLS Trail. Full details of all the *gîtes d'étape* in the area will be found at www.gites-refuges.com.

For information on the many hotels, *chambres d'hôte* and camping sites along the RLS Trail, contact local tourist offices and/or the Association Sur Le Chemin de Robert Louis Stevenson (see Appendix 5). The Parc National des Cévennes (see also Appendix 5) provides a free leaflet, Les Gîtes d'étape en Cévennes, which is regularly updated.

APPENDIX 2

OTHER LONG-DISTANCE WALKING ROUTES ENCOUNTERED ON THE RLS TRAIL

The Massif Central area of the Auvergne and Cévennes has a higher concentration and mileage of long-distance GR trails than any other region of France, a testament to the high quality of walking that can be enjoyed there. Details of the many other GR trails that are encountered while walking the RLS Trail are summarised below. Some of them are described by Cicerone guidebooks in English (e.g. GR4, GR40 and GR68), but the others are all covered by Topo guides in French, published by the Fédération Française de la Randonnée Pédestre. These guidebooks can be ordered from some outlets in the UK, e.g. the Map Shop at Upton-upon-Severn, or over the web from Au Vieux Campeur, a huge outdoor store based in Paris (see Appendix 5 for details of both).

GR430, Le Chemin de Saint-Régis

Le Chemin de Saint-Régis is a circular trail 205km (127 miles) in length, starting and finishing in Le Puy-en-Velay and exploring the regions of the Velay and Vivarais to the east. After Le Monastier-sur-Gazeille the trail, named after a 17th-century local missionary, visits Fay-sur-Lignon, Saint-Agrève, Rochepaule, Saint-Bonnet-le-Froid and Montregard, before heading back to Le Puy via Tence and Saint-Julien-Chapteuil. The first 19km of the GR430 is followed in this guidebook – from the centre of Le Puy to the start of the RLS Trail at Le Monastier-sur-Gazeille.

GR3, Sentier de la Loire

966km (600 miles) or more of footpaths following the course of the River Loire from the sea in Brittany, near Saint-Nazaire, to its source close to the Gerbier-de-Jonc, southeast of Le Monastier-sur-Gazeille. The route passes through the following regions: Océan, Brière, Anjou, Val de Loire, Orléanais, Niverais, Bourbonnais, Forez and Velay. The terrain is gentle, attractive and varied. The GR3 is encountered on the RLS Trail between Saint-Martin-de-Fugères and Goudet.

GR40, Tour du Velay

161km (100 miles) encircling Le Puy. The itinerary includes Vorey, Mont-Bar, Allègre, Siaugues-Saint-Remain, La Durande, Montbonnet, Le Bouchet-Saint-Nicolas, Goudet, Alleyrac, Les Estables, Mont Mézenc, Saint-Front, Boussoulet, Mont Meygal, Le Pertius and Saint-Julien-du-Pinet. The GR40 is encountered several times on the RLS Trail in the Velay. (My guidebook to the Tour of the Velay is available from Cicerone – see Appendix 4.)

GR4, Sentier Méditerranée – Océan

A very long west-to-east route from Royan on the Atlantic coast to Grasse above the Côte d'Azur. The route passes through the following regions: Océan, Saintonge, Limousin, Auvergne, Margeride, Cévennes, Vallée du Rhone, Gorges du Verdon and Provence. It crosses the RLS Trail at Langogne. (I have written two guidebooks for Cicerone covering the most spectacular sections of the GR4: in the Auvergne, Volvic to Langogne, and in Provence, Grasse to Langogne – see Appendix 4.)

GR7, Sentier Vosges – Pyrénées

Another ultra-long-distance route stretching from Ballon d'Alsace to Andorra in the Pyrenees. On the way it passes through the Vosges, Plateau de Langres, Côte d'Or, Mâconnais, Beaujolais, Lyonnais, Vivarais, Cévennes, Haut Languedoc, Corbières and Pyrenees. The GR7 is followed in this guidebook from the Monastery of Notre-Dames-des-Neiges to La Bastide-Puylaurent.

GR44

A 87km (54 mile) spur of the GR4, running west from Les Vans on the GR4 to Villefort, Mas d'Orcières, Col de la Loubière and Champerboux. The route passes just to the south of Le Bleymard where it crosses the RLS Trail. There are various extensions and spurs from the main trail, including the GR44A, which runs south from Les Vans to Bessèges, the GR44C, which is encountered on our route a little before Alès and runs north from there towards the Cévennes, and the GR44D, which is used in this guidebook as a walking trail from the Col d'Uglas, north of Mialet, eastwards to Alès (see Epilogue).

GR68, Tour du Mont Lozère

A circular walking tour, 110km (68 miles) in length, encircling this mountain massif in the Cévennes. From Villefort on the Paris–Nîmes railway line, the route includes Cubières, Orcières, Col des Sagnoles, Florac, Croix de Berthel, L'Aubaret, Gourdouse and Les Bouzèdes. Much of this is within the Cévennes National Park. The RLS Trail is coincident with the GR68 for nearly 11km (7 miles) from the Col de la Planette westwards to a point a few kilometres east of Florac. It can also be used as a shorter alternative to the RLS Trail into Florac (see Appendix 4).

GR43, La Draille de la Margeride

A 88km (55 mile) route following an ancient drove road (*draille*), linking the GR4 at Sainte-Eulalie to the GR7 at the Col des Faïsses, west of Barre des Cévennes. It is a harsh trail, passing through uninhabited country with little opportunity, with the exception of Florac, of finding accommodation. The route is coincident with the RLS Trail through Florac.

GRs de Pays du Causse Méjean

Those RLS Trail walkers who become fascinated with the high plateaus of the Causses, seen to the west of Florac, can become better acquainted with this unique region by taking one of the circular *GRs de pays*. The one closest to the RLS Trail is the 111km

(69 mile) long GR de Pays Tour du Causse Méjean, which can be reached by a 2km walk from Florac to the Col de Pierre-Plate on the Causse. The riot of spring flowers on the Causses is a sight not to be missed.

GR72

The GR72 links the GR4 near Le Bez to the GR7 at the Barre des Cévennes. It was followed by the old route of the RLS Trail for the 3.3km between La Bastide-Puylaurent and Le Thort, but is now met at the Maison Forestière de Champ-Long-de-Bougès, to the south of Le Pont-de-Montvert. From here the GR70 is coincident with the GR72 for a short distance to the Col de la Planette, where the RLS Trail leaves the GR72 to head west to Florac. However, the GR72 could be taken as a short cut from the Col de la Planette to Cassagnas, thereby omitting the large loop to Florac on the RLS Trail.

GR67, Tour des Cévennes

An 130km (81 mile) walking tour encircling the valleys of the numerous Gardon rivers. From Anduze the trail heads to Saint-Felix-de-Pallières and Colognac and over the Col de Asclié and the Col du Pas to Aire de Côte, east of Mont Aigoual. The path continues to L'Hospitalet, Barre des Cévennes, Plan de Fontmort, Col de Jalcreste and then south to Saint-André-de-Lancize, Mialet, Mas Soubeyran and back to Anduze. It is followed on the RLS Trail for a few kilometres from near the Plan de Fontmort, south of Cassagnas, and is also taken in this guidebook from Mialet to Aïgladines (see Epilogue).

GR67A

A variant of the GR67, it leaves the main route 3.3km to the west of the Plan de Fontmort and heads southeast to Saint-Germain-de-Calberte. It crosses the River Gardon-Saint-Germain at the Pont de Burgen before rejoining the GR67 near Saint-Martin-de-Boubaux. It is followed by the RLS Trail for several kilometres from the point at which it leaves the GR67 to the west of the Plan de Fontmort, to near the Pont de Burgen, north of Saint-Étienne-Vallée-Française.

GR61

A short trail linking two points on the GR67 – Mialet, north of Anduze, and the Col de Asclié, northwest of Colognac. In so doing, it passes through Saint-Jean-du-Gard, where the RLS Trail terminates, and is used in this guidebook to reach Mialet from Saint-Jean (see Epilogue).

E4

Sections of the GR7, GR72 and GR44 form part of the European Long Distance Path that runs from Rust in eastern Austria, across northern Switzerland and southern France, to Fredes, southwest of Barcelona in Spain, a distance of 3414km (2122 miles). The E4 passes through the Cévennes National Park from Les Vans to Villefort and on to Mont Aigoual, and then through the Haut-Languedoc Regional Park, still following the GR7.

APPENDIX 3

STEVENSON'S ITINERARY

First Day, Sunday 22 September 1878
Le Monastier-Sur-Gazeille – Saint-Martin-De-Fugères – Goudet (lunch) – Ussel –
Le Bouchet-Saint-Nicolas
Overnight in an auberge at Le Bouchet-Saint-Nicolas.

Second Day, Monday 23 September 1878
Le Bouchet-Saint-Nicolas – Pradelles (lunch) – Langogne
Overnight at inn (?) in Langogne.

Third Day, Tuesday 24 September 1878
Started after lunch, i.e. at 2.30pm (morning spent writing journal).
Langogne – Fouzilhic/Fouzilhac
RLS lost his way in the dark, so camped out overnight, 'A Camp in the Dark'.

Fourth Day, Wednesday 25 September 1878
Fouzilhic/Fouzilhac – Cheylard-l'Évêque (Breakfast/Lunch) – Luc
Overnight at inn in Luc.

Fifth Day, Thursday 26 September 26th 1878
Luc – La Bastide-Puylaurent – Notre-Dame-Des-Neiges
Overnight in a room in the monastery of Notre-Dame-des-Neiges.

Sixth Day, Friday 27 September 1878
A late start (pm), lunched with monks.
Notre-Dame-Des-Neiges – return to La Bastide-Puylaurent Chasseradès
Overnight at inn in Chasseradès, '…in the inn kitchen that night were all men
employed in survey for one of the projected railroads'.

Seventh Day, Saturday 28 September 1878
Chasseradès – L'estampe – Montagne Du Goulet – Le Bleymard (lunch) – Mont Lozère
Camped overnight at 1400 metres (4590ft) on Mont Lozère, 'A Night among the
Pines'.

Eighth Day, Sunday 29 September 1878
Mont Lozère – Pic De Finiels – Le Pont-De-Montvert (lunch) – Tarn Valley
Camped out overnight in the Tarn valley.

Ninth Day, Monday 30 September 1878
Tarn Valley – La Vernède (breakfast) – Florac (lunch)
Overnight at inn in Florac.

Tenth Day, Tuesday 1 October 1878
'A very late start', i.e. after lunch.
Florac – Tarnon – Mimente Valley
Camped out overnight in the Mimente valley, 'A little hollow underneath the oak was my bed'.

Eleventh Day, Wednesday 2 October 1878
Mimente Valley – Cassagnas (lunch) – Col De Laupies – Saint-Germain-De-Calberte
Arrived after dark and spent the night at an inn in Saint-Germain-de-Calberte,
'…I must have gone supperless to roost'.

Twelfth Day, Thursday 3 October 1878
A very late start: '…it was long past three before I left Saint-Germain-de-Calberte'.
Saint-Germain-De-Calberte – Saint-Étienne-Vallée-Française – Saint-Pierre – Saint-Jean-Du-Gard
Darkness had fallen by the time he reached the summit of Saint-Pierre. He stayed overnight at the Hotel du Cheval Blanc in Saint-Jean-du-Gard (now demolished).

Summary of Stevenson's Journey
Six nights were spent at inns/*auberges*.
Four nights were spent camping 'wild'.
One night was spent in a room in a monastery.
One night (the last) was spent in an hotel.

APPENDIX 4

BIBLIOGRAPHY

Travels with a Donkey in the Cévennes by Robert Louis Stevenson. First published in 1879, with many editions over the years. Three of the most recently published are by Quiet Vision Publishing (2002), Penguin Books (with *The Amateur Emigrant,* 2004) and Frontlist Books (paperback, 2006). There is also an audio CD version by Naxos Audio Books (1994). The continuing popularity of the book suggests that at least one version of this classic work will remain in print in the foreseeable future. The book is also published in French: *Voyage avec un âne dans les Cévennes,* Éditions du Rouergue.

The Cévennes Journal. Notes on a Journey Through The French Highlands, edited by Gordon Golding, Mainstream Publishing (1978). The previously unpublished text of the notebooks kept by Stevenson on his 1878 journey, together with later journal additions and other fragments and drawings. This journal formed the basis of *Travels with a*

Donkey. Unfortunately it is now out of print, but copies should be available from second-hand bookshops or from public libraries. The original journals are housed in the Huntington Library at San Marino, California, www.huntington.org.

Stevenson's Cévennes journal is also published in French: *RL Stevenson, Journal de Route en Cévennes*, Éditions Privat/Club Cévenol (1978). Originally published in the centenary year of RLS's journey, the latest edition is dated 2002 and, unlike its English counterpart, still in print.

Stevenson & Modestine – Voyage en Cévennes, Collection: Carnet de Voyage de Poche, Éditions des 3 Provinces. This inexpensive pocket booklet, updated regularly, is available locally and a copy should be purchased at the earliest opportunity. It contains up-to-date information and contact details of accommodation along the RLS Trail, as well as a whole range of other facilities, including restaurants, baggage-transfer services, train and bus transport, and so on, en route. There are even special boxes in the booklet for *Gîte d'étape* or hotel stamps, which can be collected while walking the trail.

Walks in Volcano Country by Alan Castle, Cicerone Press (1992). A guidebook detailing two walks in the Auvergne: i) a traverse of the High Auvergne (180km/110 miles or 260km/160 miles; 10 or 15 days) from Volvic across the Puy de Dome, Puy de Sancy and Cantal to Saint-Flour and on to Langogne, where it meets the RLS Trail; ii) the Tour of the Velay, a 160km/100 mile (8 day) circular walk around Le Puy, including Mont Mézenc and Mont Meygal. The RLS Trail encounters this walk at Montagnac and Le Bouchet-Saint-Nicolas (Stage 2).

Walking the French Gorges by Alan Castle, Cicerone Press (1993). The guidebook includes an alternative trail across the Cévennes from Les Vans, via Thines and Loubaresse to Langogne, where it meets the RLS Trail.

Walking in the Cévennes by Janette Norton, Cicerone Press (2002). Thirty one-day walks in the region, plus a guide to the GR68, the Tour du Mont Lozère.

Le Chemin de Stevenson, Fédération Française de la Randonnée Pédestre. The French Topo guide to the trail.

The Stevenson Trail in the Cévennes has spawned a considerable number of French publications, principally 'coffee-table-style' books, which British walkers able to read French may find attractive as souvenirs or as presents for friends at home. These are all available locally or, for example, in the main bookshops in Nîmes. Among the best are:

Le Chemins des Crêtes avec Robert Louis Stevenson à travers les Cévennes by Kenneth White with watercolour illustrations by Paul Moscovino, Etude & Communication Éditions (2005).

Sur les Pas de Robert Louis Stevenson – Un Voyage de Velay et Cévennes by Anne Le Maître, Éditions du Rouergue. A sketchbook with watercolours.

Voyage avec un âne dans les Cévennes, Le Faou, Éditions Alain Piazzola. A cartoon edition of the story of Stevenson's journey in 1878. Good as a present for children or for those learning French.

Downhill all the Way: Walking with Donkeys on Stevenson's Trail by Hilary Macaskill and Molly Wood, Frances Lincoln (2006). The authors spent four years visiting the RLS Trail with a series of donkeys, and were accompanied by a dog named Whiskey. Their amusing account details the cuisine, history, flora and fauna of the region.

Biographies of RLS

Robert Louis Stevenson: A Biography by Claire Harman, HarperPerennial (hardback, 2005, paperback, 2006). This major biography draws on correspondence that only recently became available.

Robert Louis Stevenson by GK Chesterton, reissued by Kessinger Publishing Co. (2005). Chesterton was fascinated by RLS and this biography is a classic.

Robert Louis Stevenson by Margaret Moyes Black, Kessinger Publishing Co. (2004).

Robert Louis Stevenson: Poet & Teller of Tales by Bryan Bevan, Rubicon Press (1993).

Many other biographies of RLS have been published over the years, but most are now out of print.

APPENDIX 5

USEFUL ADDRESSES, TELEPHONE NUMBERS AND WEBSITES

The Map Shop, 15 High Street, Upton-upon Severn, Worcestershire WR8 OHJ, freephone 0800 085 4080, www.themapshop.co.uk

Au Vieux Campeur, 48 Rue des Ecoles, 75005 Paris, www.auvieuxcampeur.fr, e-mail infos@auvieuxcampeur.fr

Nearest Metro station: Maubert-Mutualite. Extensive range of French maps and guidebooks that can be ordered online, paying by credit card.

IGN French mapping: www.ign.fr

Association Sur Le Chemin de Robert Louis Stevenson, 48220 Pont-de-Montvert, tel 04.66.45.86.31, e-mail asso.stevenson@libertysurf.fr

The association produces a free, annually updated, large folded leaflet which lists all hotels, *gîtes d'étape*, campsites and restaurants that belong to the association and which serve walkers and others along the trail. This leaflet is readily available locally or by post from the association. There are versions of these leaflets in French, English and German. The association's website www.chemin-stevenson.org – the official website for the RLS Trail – is superb and has an English option. All up-to-date information on the facilities along the trail is included, and the accommodation section has links to hotels, *gîtes d'étape, chambres d'hôte,* restaurants, and so on, so that reservations can be made online. There is even an online shop selling books, CDs and mementoes of the trail. A 'must view' site.

www.gites-refuges.com

Information on 3200 *gîtes d'étape* and *refuges* in France – use this website to find up-to-date details of the *gîtes d'étape* on the RLS Trail. There is an English option and it is possible to search by long-distance trail. Contact details for all *gîtes* and refuges are given, and there are automatic links to some *gîte* websites, allowing online booking. A book (*Gîtes d'étape de Randonnée et Refuges* by Annick and Serge Mouraret) listing all of France's *gîtes* and *refuges* can also be purchased from this site.

Baggage Transfer Services

For the RLS Trail between Le Puy, Saint-Jean-du-Gard and Alès: Transbagages, www.transbagages.com, tel 08.20.02.54.51.
Stevenson Bagages, e-mail stevensonbagages@wanadoo.fr, tel 06.87.68.35.60.

Taxi Companies

For the various stages of the RLS Trail:
Le Puy to Le Monastier-sur-Gazeille, Taxi Jean-Pierre Taulemesse, tel 04.71.08.24.52.
Le Monastier-sur-Gazeille to Le Bouchet-Saint-Nicolas, Taxi Masson-Temey, tel 04.71.03.94.36. Le Bouchet-Saint-Nicolas to Pradelles, Taxi Jean-Pierre Taulemesse, tel 04.71.08.24.52. Pradelles to Cheylard-l'Évêque, Taxi Pradelles Thierry Jourde, tel 04.71.00.87.84. Cheylard-l'Évêque to Le Bleymard, Taxi Eric Genestier, tel 04.66.47.04.66. Le Bleymard to Florac, Taxi Michel Buisson, tel 04.66.47.63.25. Florac to Alès, Taxi Michel Andre, tel 04.66.44.71.47.
These are all members of the Association Sur Le Chemin de Robert Louis Stevenson, and so can be relied upon for good service.

Donkey Hire

There are several companies offering donkeys for hire along the RLS Trail. The following are just two possibilities. Gentiane: Christine Boucher, http://anegenti.free.fr, tel. 04.66.41.04.16. Badjâne: Annie Galland, www.badjane.org, tel 04.66.56.71.54.

French Railways (SNCF)

www.sncf.com is the French site. For an English version, use www.sncf.com/indexe.htm. Timetables can be checked and reservations made on this site.

Eurostar Timetables and Bookings
www.raileurope.co.uk/eurostar/index.asp

Fédération Française de la Randonnée Pédestre
www.ffrandonnee.fr. An excellent site on all aspects of walking long-distance footpaths in France.

Club Cévenol
www.club-cevenol.org

Tourism in the Cévennes
www.Cevennes-tourisme.fr. From spring 2007 this website is available in English. It includes sections 'Where to Stay', 'What to Do', 'Where to Visit', 'Where to Walk' and so on.

Parc National des Cévennes
www.cevennes-parcnational.fr, e-mail info@www.cevennes-parcnational.fr. Some information is in English.

Local Tourist Offices
Along the route described in this guidebook there are tourist offices (offices de tourisme, or the smaller syndicats d'initiative) at Le Puy-en-Velay, Le Monastier-sur-Gazeille, Pradelles, Langogne, Le Pont-de-Montvert, Florac, Saint-Étienne-Vallée-Française, Saint-Germain-de-Calberte, Saint-Jean-du-Gard and Alès.

In the first instance contact the tourist offices at either Le Puy-en-Velay (www.ot-lepuyenvelay.fr (English option), e-mail info@ot-lepuyenvelay.fr, tel 04.71.09.38.41) or Le Monastier-sur-Gazeille (www.jeuneloiremezenc.com, e-mail jlmlemonastier@wanadoo.fr, tel 04.71.08.37.76.).

Langogne Website
www.langogne.com

Mont Lozère Website
www.lemontlozere.com

Département of Lozère and Cévennes Website
www.cevennes-lozere.com, operated by the Pont-de-Montvert tourist office.

Heart of the Cévennes Website
www.coeurdescevennes.com, operated by the Saint-Germain-de-Calberte tourist office.

Saint-Jean-du-Gard Website
www.saint-jean-du-gard.com

Alès Website
www.ville-ales.fr

Robert Louis Stevenson Club
This Edinburgh-based club's website has useful links to sites that contain information
on Stevenson's life and work – www.rlsclub.org.uk.

The Writers' Museum
This excellent museum at Lady Stair's Close, Lawnmarket, Edinburgh, includes an
extensive assortment of RLS's artefacts and photographs. For opening times phone
0131 529 7902.

National Library of Scotland.
George IV Bridge, Edinburgh EH1 1EW, tel 0131 623 3820, Stevenson website
www.nls.uk/rlstevenson/manuscripts.

RLS's Home in Edinburgh
Stevenson lived at 17 Heriot Row from 1850 to 1887. The present owners organise
functions in the main rooms and offer bed and breakfast accommodation, sleeping in
Stevenson's old room. The website www.stevenson-house.co.uk includes photographs
of Stevenson's old home and information about his life.

APPENDIX 6

MODERN TREKS ALONG
THE RLS TRAIL

The first person to follow the route taken by Stevenson in the Cévennes, and write of
his experiences, was a certain Mr Skinner, in 1926, although he made use of a motor
car. The first to walk with a donkey was a woman, Miss Elizabeth Singer, in 1948, when
she was 21 years of age.

In more recent times there have been three notable journeys along the trail. The
first was that of Mrs Betty Gladstone, an American, who walked from Le Monastier to
Saint-Jean-du-Gard in May 1963, accompanied by her 12- and 18-year-old daughters
and a donkey. She became almost a legend in the Cévennes, returning several times,
and in autumn 1965 she donated the granite plinth that was to be erected outside the
post office in Le Monastier to mark the place where Stevenson began his journey (see

Stage 1). This commemorative plaque was unveiled at a small ceremony by the late Mrs Nancy Brackett, president of the RLS Club of Edinburgh at that time, and a relative of Stevenson. (Mrs Gladstone died in 1990.)

Exactly 99 years after Stevenson had started his journey with Modestine, at daybreak on 22 September 1977, another American woman, Carolyn Bennett Patterson, set out from Le Monastier to follow in Stevenson's footsteps. She too travelled with a donkey, also christened Modestine, but this Modestine was 14 years old and somewhat larger than her predecessor. Carolyn Patterson was one of the senior editors at *National Geographic* magazine, and the story of her journey, which she made accompanied by photographer Cotton Coulson, appeared in the October 1978 issue (Vol. 154, No. 4, pp 535–61).

Carolyn Patterson tried to follow Stevenson's itinerary as closely as possible, although some changes to the route had to be made, as sections of RLS's original path were by then along fairly busy, motorable roads on which it wasn't safe to travel with a donkey. She stayed overnight at the same locations as Stevenson – where he had stayed at an inn, then so did she, and when he spent a night under the stars, she did as well. When RLS spent the morning writing up his journal before setting out, as at Langogne, then so did Carolyn Patterson. She too stayed at the Trappist monastery of Our Lady of the Snows, and like Stevenson attended compline and salve regina after dinner. Mrs Patterson finished her journey, like RLS, on 3 October, 12 days after setting out from Le Monastier.

The year after Carolyn Patterson's walk, 1978, was the centenary year of Stevenson's trek. To mark the occasion a group of six writers and outdoor journalists assembled at Le Monastier to retrace Stevenson's journey. The group was under the leadership of Rob Hunter (Neillands), a journalist and well-known writer on walking in France (who sadly died in 2006). After attending a reception hosted by the local people, the party set out early one September morning to inaugurate the newly waymarked trail. They were welcomed at various points along the route by many local people and holidaymakers, who came out in force to offer encouragement. Only seven days later the walkers arrived at Saint-Jean-du-Gard, at the end of the trail.

This centenary walk was not a complete success, however, as the temperature was very high, with blazing sunshine every day, which led to heat exhaustion for a couple of people and bad blisters for others. Moreover, they did not take a donkey, no doubt a wise decision, but instead had to carry heavy packs containing camping gear (there was very little accommodation available on the route in those days), which added to the general discomfort.

A decade later, in August 1988, I made my first journey along the RLS Trail, with further walking and research in 1989 and 1990. The result was the first guidebook in English to the RLS Trail, published by Cicerone Press in 1992. Shortly after this the French GR authority, the Fédération Française de la Randonnée Pédestre, sanctioned an official GR route for the RLS Trail, and since that time many tens of thousands of walkers, as well as cyclists and motorists, have followed in the footsteps of Stevenson in the Cévennes.

LISTING OF CICERONE GUIDES

BACKPACKING
The End to End Trail
Three Peaks, Ten Tors
Backpacker's Britain Vol 1 – Northern England
Backpacker's Britain Vol 2 – Wales
Backpacker's Britain Vol 3 – Northern Scotland
The Book of the Bivvy

NORTHERN ENGLAND LONG-DISTANCE TRAILS
The Dales Way
The Reiver's Way
The Alternative Coast to Coast
A Northern Coast to Coast Walk
The Pennine Way
Hadrian's Wall Path
The Teesdale Way

FOR COLLECTORS OF SUMMITS
The Relative Hills of Britain
Mts England & Wales Vol 2 – England
Mts England & Wales Vol 1 – Wales

UK GENERAL
The National Trails

BRITISH CYCLE GUIDES
The Cumbria Cycle Way
Lands End to John O'Groats – Cycle Guide
Rural Rides No.1 – West Surrey
Rural Rides No.2 – East Surrey
South Lakeland Cycle Rides
Border Country Cycle Routes
Lancashire Cycle Way

CANOE GUIDES
Canoeist's Guide to the North-East

LAKE DISTRICT AND MORECAMBE BAY
Coniston Copper Mines
Scrambles in the Lake District (North)
Scrambles in the Lake District (South)
Walks in Silverdale and Arnside AONB
Short Walks in Lakeland 1 – South
Short Walks in Lakeland 2 – North
Short Walks in Lakeland 3 – West
The Tarns of Lakeland Vol 1 – West
The Tarns of Lakeland Vol 2 – East
The Cumbria Way & Allerdale Ramble
Lake District Winter Climbs
Roads and Tracks of the Lake District
The Lake District Angler's Guide
Rocky Rambler's Wild Walks
An Atlas of the English Lakes
Tour of the Lake District
The Cumbria Coastal Way

NORTH-WEST ENGLAND
Walker's Guide to the Lancaster Canal
Family Walks in the Forest Of Bowland
Walks in Ribble Country

Historic Walks in Cheshire
Walking in Lancashire
Walks in Lancashire Witch Country
The Ribble Way

THE ISLE OF MAN
Walking on the Isle of Man
The Isle of Man Coastal Path

PENNINES AND NORTH-EAST ENGLAND
Walks in the Yorkshire Dales
Walks on the North York Moors, books 1 and 2
Walking in the South Pennines
Walking in the North Pennines
Walking in the Wolds
Waterfall Walks – Teesdale and High Pennines
Walking in County Durham
Yorkshire Dales Angler's Guide
Walks in Dales Country
Historic Walks in North Yorkshire
South Pennine Walks
Walking in Northumberland
Cleveland Way and Yorkshire Wolds Way
The North York Moors

DERBYSHIRE, PEAK DISTRICT, EAST MIDLANDS
High Peak Walks
White Peak Walks Northern Dales
White Peak Walks Southern Dales
Star Family Walks Peak District & South Yorkshire
Walking In Peakland
Historic Walks in Derbyshire

WALES AND WELSH BORDERS
Ascent of Snowdon
Welsh Winter Climbs
Hillwalking in Wales – Vol 1
Hillwalking in Wales – Vol 2
Scrambles in Snowdonia
Hillwalking in Snowdonia
The Ridges of Snowdonia
Hereford & the Wye Valley
Walking Offa's Dyke Path
Lleyn Peninsula Coastal Path
Anglesey Coast Walks
The Shropshire Way
Spirit Paths of Wales
Glyndwr's Way
The Pembrokeshire Coastal Path
Walking in Pembrokeshire
The Shropshire Hills – A Walker's Guide

MIDLANDS
The Cotswold Way
The Grand Union Canal Walk
Walking in Warwickshire
Walking in Worcestershire
Walking in Staffordshire
Heart of England Walks

SOUTHERN ENGLAND
Exmoor & the Quantocks
Walking in the Chilterns
Walking in Kent
Two Moors Way
Walking in Dorset
A Walker's Guide to the Isle of Wight
Walking in Somerset
The Thames Path
Channel Island Walks
Walking in Buckinghamshire
The Isles of Scilly
Walking in Hampshire
Walking in Bedfordshire
The Lea Valley Walk
Walking in Berkshire
The Definitive Guide to Walking in London
The Greater Ridgeway
Walking on Dartmoor
The South West Coast Path
Walking in Sussex
The North Downs Way
The South Downs Way

SCOTLAND
Scottish Glens 1 – Cairngorm Glens
Scottish Glens 2 – Atholl Glens
Scottish Glens 3 – Glens of Rannoch
Scottish Glens 4 – Glens of Trossach
Scottish Glens 5 – Glens of Argyll
Scottish Glens 6 – The Great Glen
Scottish Glens 7 – The Angus Glens
Scottish Glens 8 – Knoydart to Morvern
Scottish Glens 9 – The Glens of Ross-shire
The Island of Rhum
Torridon – A Walker's Guide
Walking the Galloway Hills
Border Pubs & Inns – A Walkers' Guide
Scrambles in Lochaber
Walking in the Hebrides
Central Highlands: 6 Long Distance Walks
Walking in the Isle of Arran
Walking in the Lowther Hills
North to the Cape
The Border Country – A Walker's Guide
Winter Climbs – Cairngorms
The Speyside Way
Winter Climbs – Ben Nevis & Glencoe
The Isle of Skye, A Walker's Guide
The West Highland Way
Scotland's Far North
Walking the Munros Vol 1 – Southern, Central
Walking the Munros Vol 2 – Northern & Cairngorms
Scotland's Far West
Walking in the Cairngorms

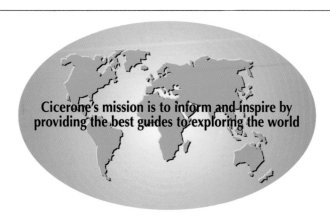

Cicerone's mission is to inform and inspire by providing the best guides to exploring the world

Since its foundation over 30 years ago, Cicerone has specialised in publishing guidebooks and has built a reputation for quality and reliability. It now publishes nearly 300 guides to the major destinations for outdoor enthusiasts, including Europe, UK and the rest of the world.

Written by leading and committed specialists, Cicerone guides are recognised as the most authoritative. They are full of information, maps and illustrations so that the user can plan and complete a successful and safe trip or expedition – be it a long face climb, a walk over Lakeland fells, an alpine traverse, a Himalayan trek or a ramble in the countryside.

With a thorough introduction to assist planning, clear diagrams, maps and colour photographs to illustrate the terrain and route, and accurate and detailed text, Cicerone guides are designed for ease of use and access to the information.

If the facts on the ground change, or there is any aspect of a guide that you think we can improve, we are always delighted to hear from you.

Cicerone Press
2 Police Square Milnthorpe Cumbria LA7 7PY
Tel:01539 562 069   Fax:01539 563 417
e-mail:info@cicerone.co.uk   web:www.cicerone.co.uk